Mr. Determination

Standing feels good. I
will not give up. I will walk.
I heard Todd speak at the
People 1st Conference and
I was inspired. I am
listening to this book on CD.
I want to share his story.

Jessie

Todd A. Presley

a.k.a
Mr. Determination

Mr. Determination

The true-life story of a sixteen-year-old
Who sustained a traumatic brain injury
And his thirty-year spiritual evolution
And his successful legal fight
To regain his right to love and independence.

PLEASE,
CHOOSE KINDNESS

Romana R. Harrison

Todd Presley and
Romana Harrison

To order additional copies of this book, visit:
www.mrdeterminationbook.com
To contact us, send an e-mail to:
mrdetermination@hotmail.com

Contents

This book is dedicated to:

Danielle, who always wanted to live in New York.

And to all those like her, whose lives are controlled by others.
May this book be an insight into what it feels like,
To live every day feeling imprisoned and with no control of your life.
I pray that this book opens the hearts and minds of all, so that we may help
each other live lives as free as we are able.

And to the people that helped me gain my freedom:

To Romana, for everything
And for introducing me to my loving volunteer, Dorothy.

To Dorothy Stearman, for all the things she did for me,
Especially finding me Bruce.

To Bruce Kimzey, my brilliant attorney
Who saw the injustice of my situation
And represented me even though I had little money at the time,
And for finding me Bill, so that I might have a house, wife, and child.

To Bill Cody,
For agreeing to be my new conservator although he had already retired
*For being how **ALL** conservators should be*
And knowing when it was time to set me free.

And to my beloved wife, Kelli,
For being an amazingly wonderful wife and mother.
Without her I would still be sad and lonely
And I would still be conserved.

And to my darling daughter Naomi,
May you bless the world with your presence.

ALIVE IN THE WORLD
By
Jackson Browne

I want to live in the world, not inside my head
I want to live in the world, I want to stand and be counted
With the hopeful and the willing
With the open and the strong
With the voices in the darkness
Fashioning daylight out of song
And the millions of lovers
Alive in the world

I want to live in the world, not behind some wall
I want to live in the world, where I will hear if another voice should call
To the prisoner inside me
To the captive of my doubt
Who among his fantasies harbors the dream of breaking out
And taking his chances
Alive in the world

To open my eyes and wake up alive in the world
To open my eyes and fully arrive in the world

With its beauty and its cruelty
With its heartbreak and its joy
With it constantly giving birth to life and to forces that destroy
And the infinite power of change
Alive in the world

To open my eyes and wake up alive in the world
To open my eyes and fully arrive in the world
To open my eyes and wake up alive in the world
To open my eyes and fully arrive in the world

Foreword by
Lynda Marinics

Founder of Choices Transitional Services

When thinking about Todd and his story, it occurs to me that there is a key theme that runs through it—that of respect; what can occur when respect is lost, and what can be created when it is retained. As a successful scholar with a promising career, it was easy for Todd to garner respect from others and to have plenty of self-respect. After a devastating life-changing event that left Todd's body shattered, his voice gone and his dreams destroyed, respect for the new being he had become was frequently hard to come by. Had he retained his family's respect, maybe this story would read differently. If our culture offered appropriate resources more respectful of someone in his situation, maybe this story would read differently, and if it were not for Todd's own self-respect, this narrative would be of a person destroyed by circumstances rather than strengthened by them.

Todd's life today is a result of his own self-respect and the love and respect of his new family—a few dedicated, respectful, and superb individuals within a flawed service system—and his own spirit of amazing strength and beauty; he just refused to give up. His tenacity, determination, intelligence, inner spirit, fire, and wonderful sense of humor have enabled Todd to create a rich and abundant life.

Congratulations, Todd, for completing this excellent narrative and making sure your voice is heard. It is my hope that this book will become a textbook in our schools, universities, and colleges—a must-read for all service providers and available in all hospital trauma units. Through such exposure, maybe others in similar circumstances will be viewed differently and will not encounter many of the almost insurmountable problems that you have faced.

I am honored to know you, Todd, you are one of my greatest teachers, my world is enriched because of you. Thank you for sharing your story and for being a part of my life.

My Foreword
By Todd A. Presley,
as Told to Romana Harrison

The reason I am writing this book is because I want to help people by letting them know that you can succeed at what others say you can't do or is impossible to do. I also want to let people know that they can break free of whatever prison they may have built for themselves, or others have built for them. To never believe that you "can't do it," whatever you may have told yourself "it" is. To let people know that love is out there, just waiting for you to find it. But you have to go looking for it; it rarely just knocks on your door.

This is also to educate families and friends of the disabled, and the public at large. When you see us out and about, know that we are people too. We have feelings; we are aware of your treatment of us. If we have someone with us, talk to us, not just to them. Even if it is in sign language, we still want to be engaged in the conversation, not left out. Don't place what *you* think our limitations are, on us. God has given us abilities you have no idea of, and we have the same rights that you do to explore and succeed at them.

This is also to educate people about the variety of agencies and services that exist for people with disabilities, my experience with them, and how they can assist or destroy life, love, and hope. There are good and bad, and I will cover them both in this book.

As for families: while most of them mean well, by doing what they think of as "protecting" us, it can often lead to control of our lives for *their* best interests, not ours. And over the years, one of my greatest sorrows has been the way that money has corrupted generally good people, and led them to do things they most likely would never have done otherwise. While cloaking it in "your best interests," it is *not* for us, but for them. I am not talking about huge sums of money either.

And this is also to inspire everyone to rise above what you may expect of yourself as well. I have lived to learn and do things that in the past I did not think I could do. Whenever you reach a goal for yourself, set a new one. Don't ever give up, don't ever take no for an answer, don't ever just settle for "good enough." As children of God, we all deserve more than that.

This book is also a special thanks for all the people that have helped me in my life. Especially Romana Harrison (My longtime Independent Living Skills Instructor and Interpreter) and Bill Cody (who later became my Conservator), whom I felt were my "adopted parents" in the way they helped me and looked out for me at a time when it felt like my own parents had abandoned me.

My attorney, Bruce Kimzey, also deserves special thanks. He was the first one to give me peace of mind by filing an ex parte order so that my stepfather couldn't take me away again without the court's permission. That was the true beginning of my freedom. Without these three people, chances are I would still be locked up in some group home and have no money, wife, child, or life.

I also want to thank Susie Davies, the head of M.O.R.E. workshop, who always stood by me, even when I didn't agree with her; Kayla, my first job coach; Vince Panto, my dear friend and boss at Super Plumbing; and Carolyn Todd, who took me to Yosemite when I most needed to get away. To Lynda Marinics, for founding Choices Transitional Services, without whom I would have never met Romana. And Valerie Walker, who has lots of courage to stand up to injustice.

I want to offer special thanks to all the medical people who also worked with me over the years. Many of their names I don't remember, but I owe them a debt of gratitude nonetheless. I do want to thank Dr. Porcella specifically for all that he did for me. He did a great job of monitoring my seizure disorder and the medications that I needed right after my accident when all this was new and very scary. I also want to thank the doctors who have worked with me since then, including Doctor Juilliard, who would see me at almost a moment's notice once I moved out on my own. My medical team has been very important to me, and I have appreciated their help and kindness over the years.

I also want to express my appreciation for ALTA Regional Center, Placerville, and my once longtime caseworker and now friend, Sally Gradall. She arranged for my closed files to be brought out of storage from Sacramento, and for the ALTA conference room to be available for the several days it took to photocopy them all.

The last reason for my writing this book is a rather selfish one. It is a form of therapy for myself, and it is a format for me to express all the pent-up thoughts and feelings I have carried around all these years. There are some of my family members who think this book is way too harsh. They have a different perspective of how things were than I did, and I am certainly willing to give them that grace. But there are court facts that back up much of what my perceptions were at the time.

No one will ever really know what it was like from my perspective if I don't write the way it felt to live it. Whatever their reality was, and whatever my perceptions were and how they differ, are still both valid. I am sorry for the pain that parts of this book may cause some of my family, and some others, but it *is* how I feel my life has been. Looking from the inside out. And if it can influence anyone to consider how their actions may affect others, then it will all have been worth it. I can only write this as I lived and felt it. I can't change what I experienced because some people don't agree with how I saw and felt about things. Then this would be their story, not mine. I'm not saying that this is logical or exactly how reality was, but it *is* what my reality was to *me*. I hope that they will be able to find it in their hearts to understand that this has been a difficult life for all of us, and I do not mean to hurt any of them. I apologize in advance for any pain it may cause, but I can only write this as I lived it, again, from my perception of my life, be it right or wrong to others.

I want people to know that parts of this book will be hard to read . . . as they were hard to write. Much of it is as difficult to read as it was to live. But that is also the very point of it all. I have to express everything that I felt, right or wrong, so that others will have some idea of what it was like to go through the experiences that I have. So that perhaps it will serve both as a warning as to what not to do, how not to treat a disabled person, and how it can strike to the very heart of feeling dehumanized and devalued as a person. For that is how I often felt with no control or say over my life. Please, please don't let this happen to anyone else!

It has also prompted me to do further research into those early days right after my accident. I have found out information I was too foggy to be aware of at that time. It has been very beneficial for me to be able to find out where I was and what was happening to me during that time. I have learned that I had more health and behavioral difficulties than I had been aware of. I would strongly encourage people to keep as many records of their accidents, medical, rehabilitation, legal, financial, and any other information for themselves as possible. They'll be glad later that they did.

Or if you have a friend or loved one that goes through something like this, if you can save as much information for them as possible, it can help to rehabilitate their memory of all that they might have lost. Over the previous couple of years, I have gotten copies of all of my past court records so that I would have a clearer vision of all of the details of my life from that time. They have been of great help to me and proved many of the things that I had thought to be so. It has been gratifying to read what my ALTA caseworkers and the court documents say because I've not been able to get any of the facts from my family. The court records in particular differ from my family's perception of how things were in regards to how my stepfather handled my money. All the time that I thought something was wrong and they disagreed with me, the court records, have in the end, shown that I was right.

This now brings me to how this book is being written. It is very much a back-and-forth between Romana and I. Even though she has helped me with the words by being my verbal thesaurus, I have chosen each word used, and we have changed many things as we have read it aloud over and over. We have discussed my life and what she has known about it on the journey she has traveled with me over the past seventeen years. She has been my memory for many years, and she has reminded me of things and subjects I wanted to make sure that I covered. I want people to know, though, that neither she nor my wife Kelli have put any of these words in my "mouth." Every word has been *my* choice. It is a severe insult to me when people say that anyone else has manipulated me into writing the book as it has become. They should know by now that I am way too stubborn and determined to let this be anyone's but *my* own story in *my* own words.

I also want to add a bit here about the cover of the book and its importance to me. I was insistent that we design it ourselves, that it have special meaning, rather than simply having someone at the publishing house design something nice, but with no particular meaning to me or my story. I wanted it to have visual impact and meaning.

The first day I met Romana, I drew a crude staircase on a piece of paper. It took a bit of back-and-forth for me to get the meaning of it across to her, which was this—I had been a bit of a butthead jock before my accident, and while a reasonably nice person, not overly compassionate to those less fortunate to me. I could be rather impatient with others and wanted things my way *now*! After my accident, I had to find a way to deal with the new me. It took many more years, but as time passed and I was not as "able-bodied" as I had been, I developed lots more understanding and compassion. I would get upset when I saw others less fortunate than I being teased for being disabled. This staircase then came to represent my spiritual growth. So I wanted Romana to know that I had grown and changed, for what I felt was the better, during this difficult existence that I had lived since the accident. That was the staircase.

When we started working on the cover, I knew I wanted it to be purple since that is my favorite color in the world. I wanted the staircase, and I wanted something to show movement up that staircase. We looked for two weeks online at all the graphics we could find, and then we settled on the staircase and the arrow. Pointing ever upwards and forwards as I hope my life will always be, and more than that, how I hope this book will inspire others to be. Always moving up and forward, to be better and kinder people.

Something else I want to mention in this foreword is the inclusion of the lyrics to Jackson Browne's song "Alive in the World" from the *Looking East* album that he released in 1996. At this time, I was finally very happy and feeling like I had overcome some huge obstacles in my life. Music was a huge part of my life and could move me like nothing else. I live, love, and *feel* music. Because I cannot speak, music has become another part of my language. I will play certain songs to people to make them aware of how deeply I feel about things. And this song . . . "Alive in the World," epitomized the feelings of my life then and now. Jackson has long been one of my all-time favorite musicians for how he can draw the deepest feelings to the surface, and this would be my favorite of all songs.

I had lived trapped by my body and inability to communicate with many. This song speaks of not wanting to live behind a wall anymore. And that is exactly where I felt I had been living for so long. As hard and painful as the world may be, I always wanted to live there, and not in some group home. This song spoke to me of being free.

I want to thank Romana's friend, Phil, who came for a visit from Hawaii a couple of years ago with an extra ticket to a Jackson Browne concert and told her to find a friend who wanted to go. Knowing how much I love Jackson's music, she immediately invited me, and it was an amazing event in my life.

So it was that I got to live the dream I'd always had of seeing him in person. It was an acoustic performance in a medium-size setting in an older venue, which made it more intimate and enjoyable. I hope to meet Jackson someday and thank him in person for bringing such joy to my soul.

I have a dream that his song will be the theme song for the movie of this book and that he'll win an Oscar for best song in a movie for that year. I also hope that Robin William's will play me in the movie as well and also get an Oscar for his portrayal of me in it. I also look forward to meeting Oprah one day and thanking her also for inspiring me. Her focus on "Don't Stop Believing" has also been a huge inspiration to me as we have reached the final weeks of writing this book. Yes, I dream big, but that's how I got as far as I have. If I had listened to the all the naysayers who said I'd never live, walk, or talk, then I'd be a sad, sorry lump somewhere. So yes, I dream big, and expect it to happen. I think that is a huge part of our lives. So, I have written this book to help and inspire all and hope its message can change lives for the better.

Lastly, but most important, this book is also an answer to the question I asked God during my near-death experience and throughout all of the horrible and difficult times afterwards. "Why did this happen to me?" This book is His answer. I firmly believe that I lived and recovered because I was supposed to write this book to help and enlighten others.

My Foreword
By Romana Harrison

Communication and Investigation
(The nuts and bolts of how this book was written)

I began working with Todd Presley in March of 1991. He was described as an angry young man that had severe temper tantrums and couldn't speak, but could hear. That he couldn't read or write either and that he spoke a "modified" sign language. He was described as "difficult, but charming." What a mix!

I was fairly new at this ILS work, having just started at it in December of 1990. I had done hospice care for several years before that, and while

I did, I did volunteer work for the El Dorado County Literacy Council and had been asked to work with the folks at Mother Lode Rehabilitation Enterprises who wanted to learn to read.

Most of the people there were developmentally disabled. I worked with a young lady there for some three years as a volunteer. After a dear friend I had been taking care of passed away from a brain tumor, I decided to look for other work. Another dear friend knew my literacy student and suggested that I would be good at working with folks with disabilities, as I seemed to have a lot of patience. She suggested I apply for a job at a local nonprofit agency, so I did. I interviewed and was hired subsequently by Choices Transitional Services in December of 1990, and began working with Todd the following March.

I went to ALTA to read his file before meeting him. It held the story of his accident, and that his goal was to move out of the group home he was living in and to move into his own apartment. Well . . . that's what I help folks do as an Independent Living Skills instructor. But I spoke little sign language at the time, and since they told me that Todd spoke his own version of sign language, (known as Todd Sign) I would just have to learn it and do my best to help him. Still, he sounded like a handful, and it was with some trepidation that I went to meet him at the group home, to do what we called a *living skills assessment*.

That was eighteeen years ago.

A lot has certainly happened during that time. But, from that first meeting, two things stand out.

First, when I asked him what he wanted most in his life, he communicated a house, wife, and children, specifically in that order.

Second, he asked for a piece of paper and a pen. He then proceeded to draw a crude staircase. When I asked him what it meant, he smiled and communicated that it was his spiritual growth. From who he had been before his accident, to who he was then. Even with all his pent-up anger (and we would soon learn he had reason to be that way) and what others would perceive as his drawbacks, Todd himself felt that he had become a much better person. That being "disabled" the way that he was had forced him to learn patience. He knew he had a lot to work on still. Todd has been relentless in his desire to evolve as much as he can in all ways in his life. Another thing that he has told me several times is that he is glad he can't talk, because he can have a short fuse, and he's glad he can't say what he feels sometimes because he knows that the part of his brain that is injured is the part that has to do with anger, and he often needs time to calm down and be more rational. He has always apologized for those times when the anger got the better of him.

Because of the severity of Todd's short-term memory loss, I have been his memory for many of the things that have happened in his life, since I have been working with him. Carrying it around for him became challenging at times, and when he decided he wanted to write this book, I was very glad for the chance to be able to put down on paper all that I had had to remember for him. Now, he will always have it for himself and his family.

The creation of this book has comprised primarily of two parts.

Communication and Investigation. How it was written, and how we have researched and investigated to have as many facts as accurate as possible for this.

Communication:

How does one write a book with someone who cannot speak or write? With lots of patience.

And a sincere appreciation for online thesauruses. You see, even though Todd can't speak, read, or write, he has an excellent mind, and he did have a 3.8 grade average in high school before his accident. He wasn't an avid reader, but he did enjoy books and had an excellent vocabulary. And I think that, also, by living a life in which he has had to listen so much, he has also learned many other words and continued to improve his vocabulary.

Another aspect to the way this book has been written is that every word of it has all been read aloud to Todd as it's been written. When we were working on a part, I would write the concept or point we were trying to get across then read it to him. Sometimes it was right on, and other times he wanted it tweaked some. I would highlight a word and read him all the options, and then he would choose which one he felt suited best and that would be it. Then, as we would refresh each part and I would read it again, it would also evolve. What he had liked one way at one time, as time had passed, would then strike him as needing to be different now.

We have been working on this book for about seven years now. The communication and making sure that each word written here is exactly as Todd has wanted it to be has been of paramount importance.

Now I will admit that I am a very avid reader, which has been helpful to Todd's book because it has certainly helped stretch my vocabulary. It's easy to use familiar words over and over again, but when you are writing a book like this, you need to be sure that you vary things some.

Investigation:

And then, how does one write a life story of someone who can't remember their life? In Todd's case, it came down to photocopying every piece of paper we could find that had to do with Todd's life. In his case, much of that comes from ALTA Regional Center, whose diligent caseworkers have given Todd the gift of most of it. Everything that happened from the time of his accident up to now has been dutifully documented. Every phone call his mother ever made, each visit to him, his work and health—they wonderfully kept track of everything. And it is photocopies of those volumes and volumes of files in which the puzzle of Todd's life has been found from the most human perspective. The various courts have held the framework of his legal life. From the hospital records of his accident that fateful day on August fifth of 1978, to the much later dissolving of his conservatorship case.

Much of Todd's own history he didn't know, and only came to learn it via the ALTA or court documents.

Ever since Todd moved into his own apartment, he began keeping binders with all the correspondence or documents he ever received. He organized them by date and neatly numbered the pages, and they were perfectly filed. That became the basis for later research. So each time we have embarked on a new investigative aspect of his life, he has created a new binder for it. This book even has its own binder. There are a total of seven binders that we have used for the research of this book. They are copies of all of the court documents in regards to Todd from the Stanislaus County and El Dorado County courts, as well as all of his files from ALTA Regional Center and the forensic accounting that the court ordered during his change of conservatorship hearings. And then there is Todd's personal binder. It contains letters, pictures, cards, and court documents. We have studied every page of every binder many times.

As we wrote, we would find the places in the binders that corresponded to the time frame that we were working on to be sure dates and facts were as accurate as possible. Again, we got the bones from the court binders, and the filling for much of it from ALTA.

Todd also wanted this book to be about more than just his life. He wants this book to really help people. That's one reason he talks about the different programs that are available, as well as things that happened in his life, while talking about the places he's lived in and the situations he came across, and how humans and bureaucrats handled them differently. The difference was where the "rule of law" was more important than the person suffering to the individual handling the "case."

This book has taken a long time to investigate. We often had to wait extended periods for the needed court documents to come in, and some we have had to go to print without. But Todd is happy with what we have, and his goal is to have this published by the beginning of 2010.

I have been accused in the past of keeping Todd from his family, or trying to sway him in some way. Those that know Todd knows that's not possible if it's something he feels strongly about. He has offered to send me on my way if I pushed a view that he did not care for very much, but he always told me the reason. Mostly it was about my wanting him to be close to his mother, but he has remained upset that she thinks we manipulated him. But for the record, I never ever tried to stop him. It was always the opposite situation; I always wanted his family to be close to him, for him to have a warm and loving relationship with them. It is and always will be Todd's choice.

Lastly . . . meeting and knowing Todd has been an amazing experience in perseverance. He has worked and struggled to get to where he is now. He was determined to never give up, and he hasn't. He is a wonderfully kind and loving man in spite of how he could have become angry and bitter. Instead, he does all he can to make this world a better place as best he can.

It has been a wonderful challenge to write this book with Todd for the past seven ought years, and like him, I hope it opens many minds and hearts to be more inclusive to all people.

Todd is, indeed, Mr. Determination, and it's a true spiritual blessing to call him my friend.

Chapter 1

My Life Before the Accident
(My goals and dreams, who I was)

August 1978. It was the summer before my senior year of high school. I worked hard to maintain a 3.8 grade average. I enjoyed school very much. I was on the water polo team as a goalie. I played tennis. I was a photographer for my high school yearbook. I was a popular, good-looking jock with a girlfriend. I was working part-time at a veterinarian's office. They liked me there and said I did good work. I planned to go to UC Davis to get a degree to be a veterinarian when I graduated. The whole world was before me, and I knew I could succeed at anything I set my mind to. I was in great physical shape with an excellent sense of balance. In 1976, I was in the bicentennial Fourth of July parade in Modesto. I wore a Stars and Stripes outfit, rode a unicycle, and bounced a basketball around me in circles while riding down the street in the parade.

I lived with my mother and my stepfather, my twin sister Cindy, and my younger half sister Sara, who was twelve years younger. I also had an older sister, Stephanie, who was seven years older than I, and an older brother, Scott, who was five years older. Lou had a son, Steffen, who was eleven years older than I was. The older siblings had all moved out by this time. And it was just Cindy, Sara, and me at home.

I had been born in NYC, and my parents moved to California when I was around six. My mother says that they separated shortly after that. She doesn't say when they divorced or when she met Lou, so I am unsure of many facts. I think my mother married Lou not long after we moved to California. My perceptions of Lou Presley at the time were that he was a wonderful dad who loved my siblings and me very much. He was very supportive and proud of me for my academic and sports accomplishments. He was a good role model for me as well as in other ways.

Romana has asked me if the sixteen-year-old Todd would ever have believed that Lou could become the person that he later did, and I wouldn't have. I would have thought that he was too honest, loving, and loyal to have turned into what he did in later years. But that is also a part of this book. How money and power can change someone from a really good person to someone corrupt. The person he later became to me sadly overshadows the good feelings I had about him for those years. My siblings still think the world of him to this day.

This is perhaps the strongest warning I can give to family and caretakers of the disabled. I loved Lou very much at that time. He was a good and stable role model, and I was very proud to have him as my father at the time. Those are my general feelings about him. I wish that I could remember more about those days, as perhaps it would lend more balance to what happened later. He worked as an accountant for Stanislaus Foods, a food manufacturing company. When they married my mother and Lou changed my name from Todd Walter Kamm to Todd Andre Presley. My mother says that I really wanted to have my name be Lou, but they talked me into just sharing his middle name. But for the life of me . . . I don't think so. Maybe, I'll be honest and say I don't remember that time at all, but I do know that I liked my name Todd. I was never formally adopted nor did they ever legally change my name, but I did become Todd Andre Presley and Lou's son from then on.

I have had people tell me that I am being unfair to my family by not dwelling more on the good times before things got difficult. But in adding up the years, at best, Lou was a **great** dad for nine years. It's true that I had a wonderful childhood with Lou as my dad. I'll be honest and say that I have few memories for five years after my accident, but I'd be willing to say they were okay. Until the money got in the way, and then it got pretty darn awful from *my perspective* for the next nineteen years. I was an adult then, so that *is* what I remember most. I can't help that. And, as you will read, I *do* have factual information from the court, repeatedly about how he had total disregard for me and my money, and the court's rules. Some of Lou's own letters also show his disregard for me, but that will reveal itself in time here.

My biological father had his own personal problems, and he was never involved in my life after we moved to California. I was later told he died in San Francisco, as did my brother Scott in separate incidents.

Chapter 2

The Accident, August 5, 1978
(How it happened, I argue with God, trapped in my body)

On August 5, 1978, I had just finished my work at the veterinarian's office and was riding my moped home. People didn't wear helmets when they rode mopeds then. Just like they didn't wear them for bicycles. I was coming to an intersection and saw a truck also coming to the intersection. I don't remember much after that, except somehow the truck hit me and I went flying up into the air, and I remember crashing down on my head.

I then found myself someplace that I knew was not "normal" life. I knew this because I did remember hitting my head and I somehow just "knew" that I was dead. I was in the presence of what I would call God. I assumed it was God, because I assumed that I was dead, and who else would be there in the afterlife if I was dead? I didn't see anything, I could only feel. And I only felt one thing, and that was enormous rage. I was aware that I was dead and all I was losing by being dead at such a young age, with all my plans before me. I could only feel fury as I asked Him again and again, "Why?" This "why?" was not as in "Why is this happening to me?" but as in "*Why in the hell are you doing this to me?*" I was blaming Him for taking me from my life at such a young age. I was only sixteen! I don't remember any answer, and in reality, the answer (if there was one) was irrelevant to me because I was so infuriated I couldn't and wouldn't hear or feel anything else. I was vaguely aware that the Presence was trying to communicate something to me, but again, I was just too full of rage to hear or feel anything from It. I blocked out whatever it was. I ranted and raved and demanded to come back and be allowed to continue my life, as I had so many things I still wanted to do on this earth. I was aware that this was agreed to and that I would be sent back. Romana has asked me if I remember anything at all from that experience. Was there light? Were there others? Do I remember anything else at all? My answer to all of that is no, no, and yes. I later remembered upon my conversations with Romana that I was sent back for a reason and that there was something I was to do, but at that time, I blocked all memory out. I was just so furious that all I wanted was to come back, and so, I was sent back. I was both stubborn and egotistical at the time, and I guess I just figured then that if I demanded to be sent back, that I would be and that everything would be exactly the way it was when I left. I had no real concept of what had actually happened to me and my body and what the repercussions would be. Romana has asked me: if God had shown me shown me how difficult my life would be, would I still have chosen to come back? And my answer is yes. I would have figured that I could and would beat whatever it was that had happened to me. I have no inclination as to how long any of this took. Imagine being in the strongest temper tantrum imaginable; well, that was the state of my mind at the time.

My next recollection was being very fuzzily awake in my body in the hospital but not being able to move or speak or communicate or open my eyes. And I was in enormous pain all over.

I was told later that they had defibrillated me three times before they got a heartbeat. As I said, my next awareness was that I was conscious in my body, while I appeared to be in a coma to everyone else. I could hear their voices, but I couldn't feel anything but pain, nor could I move or let anyone know I was aware. To them, I appeared to be unaware. This was extremely *frustrating*! I was screaming in my mind to them that I was awake, but I couldn't tell them that I was in lots of pain. I could hear them talking all around me, but I was frozen in my body with no way to communicate. I have no idea how long this state lasted. I wanted desperately to communicate with people, but I could not.

Upon researching my medical conditions, this is what I have found was my diagnosis:

I had multiple severe injuries. I had sustained a deep bruise in the left frontal lobe of my brain, as well as multiple fractures, and I had blood in both of my lungs. I underwent two brain surgeries during which they drilled holes in my skull to drain the blood that was causing pressure and swelling on my brain. This involved the left frontal regions. They also used a camera to explore my ankle internally, and then they set the two fractures that had shattered it. They had to put metal pins in it to keep it stable. I still have them to this day.

I wore a cast on my right leg for eight weeks, a cast on my right arm for eight weeks, and an arm splint after that for six months. I was also forced to wear a helmet to protect my head during all of my hospital stay. I must have been quite a sight with two of my limbs immobilized and a helmet.

Because of the injury to the left side of my head, my right arm was affected much the way a stroke victim's is. This caused an inability to be able to manipulate my arm and hand. I have feeling in it, but I have only minimal movement with it. And no fine motor dexterity.

I then developed severe breathing problems and required a tracheostomy and respiratory support for a period of time. In other words, they had to cut a hole in my throat for me to breathe through. They inserted a tube in the hole in my throat, which was then hooked up to a breathing machine. This machine breathed for me when I could not breathe for myself. I was later to learn that it was this procedure that saved my life, but might have caused the loss of my voice through the destruction of my vocal cords. We are not sure about this however, and it could be the severe damage to my brain that had also affected my ability to speak. I was still in a coma when this happened and was completely unaware of it at the time.

Subsequently, my breathing status stabilized and the tracheostomy tube was removed once I could breathe on my own. This was after I awoke from the coma, so I was on the breathing machine for at least sixty days. I was very glad when they finally did take the tube out, as it was very uncomfortable and limited my movement.

I also sustained a bleeding stress gastric ulcer. This is normally caused by mental or emotional stress, but is sometimes caused by the body suffering a severe shock from a serious injury such as I sustained. Since I was unconscious when I developed the ulcer, this seems to be the most likely answer. I had a draining tube in my side because of this, and I still have the scars from it today.

At some point, I woke up. I had no idea where I was or what had happened, or that I had been in a coma for about sixty days. I was in what I would call a very blurry condition for a long time. At some point during this stretch, I vaguely began to realize how really serious my condition was, and that my life was going to be different now. I think they told me that I might never walk again. I was in the hospital bed for what seemed like forever! Many of these things I don't remember clearly.

Chapter 3

Rehabilitation
(The long road back)

I remember being crazy furious because I still could not move. In my mind, I kept demanding an answer from God over and over. "Why did *you* do this to me? I didn't do anything to deserve this! I had so much to live for, I worked hard and made good grades . . . why, why, why?" which was my feeling at the time. I was still so very irate at Him. But there was still no answer yet. In fact, the answer would not come for many years.

When I had awoken, I realized that I was in agonizing pain in three places on my body, my head, my right arm, and right ankle. I had the world's worst headache. My ankle, as I mentioned in the last chapter, I later learned had been broken in two places, and they had had to put metal pins in it to keep it stable. My right arm had atrophied into a locked position against my body during the coma. The rehabilitation to make it work again was very painful. I have no memory of the people that were helping me. I was too upset with everything and everyone as well, as my memory was not working at that time. I also learned that my tongue and jaw were severely damaged. This had affected my ability to eat to a minor degree as well. It has gotten better as the years have gone by.

After the bed, I was put in a wheelchair. I think I remember trying to go home while I was still in the chair and had an IV drip attached. Someone from the hospital found me trying to "escape" and brought me back. I felt like "Shucks, I got caught." I was really sick of the hospital by then and ready to get out by any means necessary.

The documentation from the hospital states that I was originally admitted to Doctors Hospital in Modesto on the day of my accident, August 5, 1978. The doctors say that I awoke from my coma approximately two weeks before my transfer to Ralph K. Davies Medical Center in San Francisco on Oct 16, 1978. That would be seventy-one days. I was discharged from San Francisco on December 20, 1978 (about two months later) with an "improved condition." I was then discharged home to the care of my family at this point. This was a very fuzzy year in my memory. I don't really remember anything in particular that happened during this time except my learning to walk again. I do remember my feelings though. Time had no meaning to me. From my viewpoint, I was severely crippled and I was still full of rage. It turns out the part of my brain that was damaged were the parts where anger is centered. It was like someone was pushing down my anger button all the time, in addition to my being angry and confused at what had happened to me. I still had no idea that the injury was permanent.

From my perspective it was hell. I could not walk. I could not talk. I was not the person I had expected to be at this point in my life. I was still raging on the inside and out. As I slowly came to a confused awareness, I realized that if I didn't at least try to get out of the wheelchair, I would never know if I might walk again. My feet and legs had feeling, so they were not dead. I was and am a very stubborn individual. I wanted to get out of that chair more than anything else. I was determined to try to walk. I struggled to get out of it many times; each time I could not get out of it frustrated me into trying it again. Finally, one day, I did succeed at getting out of the chair. I wobbled a bit but somehow managed to stay on my feet. I was so full of fury and hate at the chair that I wished I could have thrown it right out of my life for good. While I had to accept that I could not talk, I would not accept that I could not walk. After I got out of the chair, I staggered on my feet to my mother and showed her that I was walking, although I was very unstable. She got intensely angry with me. She was understandably afraid of my falling down and hurting myself. I was determined that I would not live my life in that chair if I didn't have to. I knew that doctors could be wrong and I knew they were wrong about me. I don't know how I knew, but I did. Somehow I knew that if I continued to struggle, I would be able to walk again. She told me to get back in the chair. I didn't really want to, but I agreed that I would use the wheelchair just while I worked on learning to walk once again. I remember staggering from wall to wall, object to object, to give me something to hold on to. Sometimes I grabbed something that was not very stable and I fell down. But I would not let that defeat me. I struggled back up again. Slowly I did regain my balance and my ability to walk. I don't know how long this process took. Rage was my motivator.

At this point in time, I have to take a break from this narrative and say that writing this part is very difficult. I find myself feeling angry all over again, and it's very hard to go back to that point in time. I was so filled with anger that having to relive it for the sake of this book was almost enough to make me stop writing it. But I am being badgered by my wife and friends to continue for the sake of all the people this might help. So, suffice it to say, life was a nightmare back then.

My documentation shows that in August of 1979, about a year after my accident, my mother signed me up with Valley Mountain Regional Center. To me, this meant just another round of rehabilitation therapy programs. I would have no idea of what having Regional Center services would mean to me in the future and how much help they could really be.

On October 29, 1979, I first went to Santa Clara Valley Medical Center to continue my rehabilitation. I was there for 2½ months of intensive therapy. This is where I got the rehabilitation to help me learn to walk again, and they helped me rehabilitate my arm so that I could use it again. I'm afraid that having temper tantrums became something of a norm for me there. But the staff was understanding and very patient with me. They understood how mad I was, and they wanted to help me get back as much of my life as they could, and that meant the use of my arm and legs. As a part of the rehabilitation, they had me making ceramic chess pieces. I enjoyed doing that, as it gave me something productive to do. In the end, I got to keep the set that I had made, and by the time I had finished the chess set, my arm was much better.

I lived in a board and care home while I was in Santa Clara. I remember my ALTA caseworker driving me there. My documentation says her name was Elizabeth Oakes. I don't know where she is right now, but I am very grateful for the help that she gave me. She was an extremely nice person and helped me through some difficult times. I hope that wherever she is, she might have a chance to read this and know how grateful I am for her help.

When I returned to Modesto, I lived at the Parks Residential Facility Transitional Men's Home. Romana has asked me if I liked it there. I gave her the sign for feeling like being in jail. Although I did not like it, I did need to be there, and they did their best to help me. I would guess that I was pretty darn difficult to work with back then. I was still mad at everything. But again, in retrospect, I appreciated their help and patience.

My interaction with my family was extremely supportive and close. My mother was very involved in trying to procure proper services for me and in working jointly with the Regional Center to come up with a good rehabilitation plan for me. They worked very hard at encouraging me to become as independent as I could.

I was learning to use something called a Bliss Symbol Communication board to communicate. I had to learn to understand single words and use the Bliss symbols to form simple sentences. I then had to learn to combine Bliss symbols for words that were not on my board. I hated the speech therapy, especially after they said that I had a poor chance of improving my ability to speak well. In other words, I would never be able to speak like I had, and I didn't see the point in pursuing speech therapy.

Emotionally, things were very difficult. I had depression over my present physical condition. This depression at times caused me to express suicidal thoughts. In addition to my depression, I experienced a high degree of anger and frustration because of my inability to communicate my thoughts and feelings accurately. Sometimes I could get part of an idea across, but most of the time it was very frustrating. Because I couldn't write or talk, I had no outlet of expression other than the barest of rudimentary articulation. I had always been able to express myself very well, and to find myself unable to now, either with words or writing, was incredibly exasperating. Imagine if your whole life was like a warped game of charades, and that is the only way you could communicate and that was your only outlet for trying to explain your thoughts and feelings. That is how it was for me. I felt like I had dropped from being at the top of the communication scale to having almost none. And even worse than that, people were trying to guess what I was saying and were often guessing wrong, and that just got me even more discouraged. And that was only half of the equation. Because the other half was also my understanding them now. Because my brain still wasn't working right, I couldn't always understand what people were saying to me, either. Especially if they talked too fast or used words that I knew that I had used to know but somehow seemed just beyond my grasp of understanding now. It was very much like being in a foreign country where some of the time I didn't understand them and most of the time they didn't understand me. But for me, there was no translation dictionary to get my point across, and I had to live with simply not being able to express myself or communicate. Add that to all of my new physical limitations and multiply this by twenty-four hours a day, and you get the barest glimmer of how challenging this new life of mine was to me now.

I was also sometimes placed in situations where my impaired memory caused me to forget where I was going or what I was supposed to do. I expressed my frustration by pounding my feet, pounding the table, yelling, running from a situation, throwing objects, or sometimes destroying things. In order to help me cope with these feelings of frustration and anger, I began seeing a counselor from Stanislaus County Mental Health, Al Pevehouse. Al was a great help to me and was able to help me understand my situation and deal with it better emotionally.

As a side note:

For many years, anger and frustration in my life was to be a constant theme. I would, as stated above, express my anger and frustration in fairly negative ways. In later years it was still a problem even after therapy. Then one day, Romana and I came up with a workable solution. She realized that I needed to have a way to externalize my pent-up inner emotions. So she suggested that I use an exercise machine I had gotten. She said that when I felt really mad, for me to get on the machine and use it until I was exhausted and all the anger was gone. It's amazing how well this has worked! I wish I had known this years ago! Instead of tearing a dresser apart, I could have worked it out on my machine. If the workshop and group homes I was in had had such a machine, I could have taken a time-out there and worked the anger out of my system, so it was externalized instead of just causing me to boil over with violence. Since my right arm has been the weaker one, Romana specified that I could use this opportunity to turn the negativity of my anger into a positive therapeutic experience. As a result of lots of anger, my arm has gotten much stronger. Added to my frustration was the fact I could not express my feelings. After I was exhausted on the exercise machine, that didn't matter so much anymore and I felt much better. It was a win-win situation. I got rid of anger and stayed in good shape. I used the negative emotions for a positive outcome. So I would suggest that group homes and workshops have some sort of exercise machine where a frustrated or angry client can take a time-out and use it to work their anger out. I would also suggest that people who have problems with anger or frustration, for whatever reason, also have some sort of exercise machine that they can use to work their anger out in their own home. If they feel angry with a family member or something that has happened, go work it out on your machine before you say the wrong thing and hurt someone. You'll feel better and you won't have hurt someone's feelings.

Now, back to our story . . .

A bit more detail about my problem with my understanding people. I also had a processing delay in my brain that made it hard for me to understand what people were saying to me sometimes, especially if they spoke fast and in long sentences. I furthermore needed help in improving my memory deficits. I had some problems remembering my daily schedule, like where and when I was supposed to be going to appointments. Do you have any idea how frustrating that is? To know that you are supposed to go somewhere, but you just don't remember where or when? Maybe later in life, but not in your teens! I was accused at one point of "blowing it" by missing the dial-a-ride busses and not keeping track of my schedule. Well, it's hard to remember to look at your schedule when no one reminds you to look at it. I didn't do this on purpose as some folks seemed to think. My brain had been pretty well-scrambled, and this was just over a year after my accident. I am not making excuses here, just stating biological facts!

As a quick side note, Romana and I have just discussed watches with alarms, and she has asked me that if I had had such a watch to remind me to look at my calendar for instance, would that have worked. She asked me if I would have remembered that the beep meant to look at my calendar, and I am sure that it would have. So this may be a way to help others with memory problems. Much of this book will be about solving some of the problems that I had in the past to help others in the future.

Back to my story. I was still having sight problems as well. I had severe right field loss in both eyes. 60 percent in my right and 65 percent in my left. Special consideration had to be given during my cognitive training in how visual input was presented to me because of this. In other words, if it wasn't right in front of me, I couldn't see it to learn it.

At this point in time, I was pretty well able to take care of my personal hygiene and dressing skills. I had independent living training that had emphasized basic money management, concepts of apartment living, cooking skills, and shopping: i.e. for personal items, clothing, and groceries. I also had training in mobility and basic house maintenance. I was doing my own laundry and learning to take care of myself as independently as possible.

While I was at Santa Clara, I was sent to see a new neurologist because of what was believed to be focal seizures that I was experiencing off and on during my day. I was on Dilantin daily for seizure control. They adjusted my medication so that I was stabilized. This may also account for my losing track of time sometimes, because I was unaware I was having these seizures and I would find myself simply feeling rather disoriented and not knowing I'd just had a seizure, but I did feel like I had missed something, but had no idea what. After I was put on the meds, those feelings of losing time and disorientation seemed to be better.

As far as school goes, I had wanted to graduate with my twin sister, Cindy, and my senior class. I got tutoring at home from my government teacher while I strived to reach that goal. After further testing and as reality set in, it became evident that my injury was just too severe for me to be able to continue at my school, so I was transferred to Beyer High School. I was at first gravely disappointed to not be able to graduate as I had always planned, but I finally came to agree with the rest of my support team. I was enrolled in a Beyer High School orthopedically handicapped class and interacted with other students in that setting. I was also involved in biweekly group meetings for other young adults who had been involved in accidents that have been life changing. The only times I had problems socially was when I became frustrated either because of my poor memory skills or my inability to communicate my wants and needs to those around me.

I especially want to thank my support team at Beyer High: Corky Meinhart, my teacher; Jan Davis, speech therapist; Jim Tempher, acting principal; Brian Strong, speech therapist intern; Jeanette Rosenthall, reading specialist; Dick Simontor, coordinator of EAS; and Diane Lowery, the school nurse. Because of their understanding and patience with me during an exceptionally difficult time in my life. They were the best and hung in with me through thick and thin.

I finally graduated high school in June of 1980 from Beyer High School. I did not get to graduate with my sister and friends in 1979, but nonetheless, the one-year delay was not too bad, considering what I had gone through.

I also want to make short mention here of my caseworkers at Valley Mountain Regional Center. My intake worker was Derk Waring, who did quite a bit of work for my family and myself even before it was decided that I was eligible for services, and I thank him for that! My next caseworker was Elizabeth Oakes. As I said previously, she was wonderful!

There is another point I should make here. That during this time, I had rationalized that I was "special" because of what had happened to me. Because of this, I expected special treatment. I did not make some very good decisions during this time. One of my worst was shoplifting some small items from a local drugstore. I had rationalized that the world owed me something. Well, once I found myself down at the police station, I got quite a rude awakening and realized I wasn't quite as "special" as I thought I was. That's when I realized that no matter what had happened to me, I would still be held responsible for my actions. It scared me pretty bad, and I'm glad I hadn't done anything worse. So let this be a warning to you out there . . . no matter what happens to you, or how "special" you think you may be, you still have to abide by the laws, and yes, you can still get arrested. I was lucky that they decided to drop the charges that time. Narcissism (or self-centeredness) is a pretty strong trait of many of those with brain injuries, and I realize that in retrospect, I took it to extremes sometimes. I never meant to be unreasonable. It seemed pretty reasonable to me that I should be the center of "The World," after all, I was the center of *my* world, and I expected everyone else to know that. My surprise was finding out that I was only one small part of "The World." I would come to realize this more appropriately as time went by and I did not have to focus quite so much on myself. I hope that my sharing of this experience will allow other folks with brain injuries to know this and be aware of it, and their families as well. We don't mean to be as self-centered as we may seem, but it takes a lot of energy and work to keep oneself in perspective. And sometimes a rough awakening is useful, as long as it's not too serious. Romana has asked me as we work on this, if having a police officer talk to me before it got this far would have been of any help. I have told her no, that I would have realized it was "just a talk" and blown it off. It took it *really* happening to me for me to realize the severity of it and take it seriously.

So I would recommend (as someone who has been through it) that if someone is in this situation, to go ahead and have him or her arrested and taken down to the police station. Let them sit there and stew about it for a while and be in fear of what might happen before you rescue them. Let them get the full benefit of the experience so that it will have a maximum impact. That's what it took for me to really get it through my head. I don't think I ever did it again after that. I wouldn't say you need to go as far as to have them booked or spend the night, but certainly long enough the let them think that they might. And don't let them think they got off because of their disability either. Make sure they are told that the next time, they won't be rescued.

By the time two years had passed, I was still having uncontrollable temper outbursts. Even when I knew that my outbursts were causing problems for myself and those around me. I simply could not stop. Again, it was as if someone was always holding down my anger button. From the moment I got up in the morning to when I went to sleep at night, it was always on. Just like a light switch left on and the light shines, my anger button was on and the anger was on.

An example of how my anger directly affected my life was my return to my prior workplace. I was again working at the veterinarian's office where I had been before my accident. I was very happy to be there. I was not, however, able to do some of the medical procedures I had done before, and now I was "just" a kennel boy. I was very aware that I was not able to do some of the jobs I had done before. This, combined with my anger button and communication difficulties, and challenges understanding what people were saying to me, caused me to have major temper outbursts at work. I remember that I had also developed a deep belief that my life was tied to the veterinary clinic. I believed that God only let me live to work with animals in a veterinary hospital. Therefore, if I was not working in a veterinary hospital, there was no reason for me to live. I know now that this is quite unreasonable, but back then, only two years out from my accident, I was not thinking clearly. That, combined with my young age, had me convinced that I *knew* what was so. Because of my temper outbursts, the veterinarian had to let me go. My support team was very concerned and had set up appointments with my mental health counselor, Al Pevehouse, for me to see him directly before and after my termination. All in all it was a catch-22. I wanted to go back to work there, but there was no way I could have succeeded because of my uncontrollable anger and everything else. I would not have listened to my team if they had tried to tell me this. I had to experience it myself. Romana and I have discussed at length the pros and cons of my going back to that particular vet hospital, and if I might have been more successful at one I had not been to before for a fresh start. While being in a place where I could not do some of the things I could do before made it even more painful, I think that the staff was more lenient with me because they did know me. Either way, I don't think I would have been successful, but again, I had to try. It would have only made me rage more to be denied the chance to try, and I needed the lesson to learn it for myself. The only thing that might have made a difference is that if there had been a medication that I might have been able to take, that would have lessened my anger. I know those didn't exist back then, but I would like to suggest it as a viable possibility now. I would have taken it if it had existed and it could have made a profound difference in my life. I should note that in addition to my uncontrollable anger, I was also sometimes unwilling to follow instructions concerning things that I did not particularly want to do. This is another common reaction of a traumatic brain injury. Some of this had to do with so much of my life being out of my control, and by refusing to do something, that gave me a tiny sense of being in control of *something*. Sometimes there was something I wanted to do that was unreasonable, and sometimes there were things my support team wanted me to do that I didn't want to do. So, I could refuse to do what they wanted me to, and again, that gave me a sense of being in control. I never did it just to be obnoxious (although I'm sure they thought I was sometimes); it was just my way of trying to make up for all that I had lost by being in control of something. I realize that I made some really bad choices back then, but at least they were *my* choices.

Another thing that was going on was my schedule and the sheer number of people that were involved with it. I had all kinds of teachers, therapists, social workers, counselors, doctors, etc. It seemed as if I always had to remember to go to some appointment somewhere to see someone to do something. It felt like "and, and, and, and, and . . ." I had a hard time with my short-term and long-term memory. People would get upset at me for forgetting appointments. ***Hello people . . . my memory does not work***! How do you expect me to be in all these places when I don't remember? They did give me an appointment book sort of thing to remind myself, but because of my memory loss, I would forget to look at it. So that added lots of stress to me. I had been diagnosed with aphasia, which I still have.

(***Note*** about Aphasia; **Aphasia** (or **aphemia**) is a loss of the ability to produce and/or comprehend *language*, due to injury to brain areas specialized for these functions. It is not a result of deficits in sensory, intellect, or psychiatric functioning, nor due to muscle weakness or a cognitive disorder.

Depending on the area and extent of the damage, someone suffering from aphasia may be able to speak but not write, or vice versa, or display any of a wide variety of other deficiencies in language comprehension and production, such as being able to sing but not speak. Aphasia may co-occur with speech disorders such as *dysarthria* or *apraxia* of speech, which also result from brain damage.)

So, I had and, to some degree, still have this difficulty processing language. This makes it very difficult to process verbal information. I needed it written down, but I couldn't read beyond simple words and very short sentences. So, it was another catch-22. I didn't understand verbal, and I couldn't read long instructions. Wouldn't that frustrate you? I couldn't be expected to remember on my own because of my short-term memory loss. Because of all this, plus my anger button being on all the time, in addition to being frustrated with my communication and memory difficulties, I reached the point where I didn't want any more therapy of any kind. I wanted things to be simplified so I could get a grip on my life. I just wanted to work and settle into my life. I had been in a state of constant change for the two years following my accident. For two years, I had been in and out of hospitals and in and out of therapy.

After graduation, I began working full time at the HTC vocational program. As I said, at this point in time, I just wanted to be left alone and focus on working for a while. I was sick of doctors, therapists, and everything else. I also know that I had been disruptive to my family when I was not engaged in a full-time activity. I would stop by the house and expect to be the center of attention. I didn't really realize that's what I was doing at the time, but it was. I needed to get some distance from my family, for both them and me. I would go visit on Sundays, but that was about it. My mom was still involved in helping with my case management. It should be noted that I was on SSI during this time, receiving $288 per month. It cost me $438 per month to live at the facility I was at, and my parents made up the difference, for which I am very grateful,

For the next year, my life was much simplified and I began doing much better. I had fewer temper outbursts and was able to learn more things at work. I was able to learn to cook a simple dinner. I was feeling like I was finally having some control of my life and making progress.

It is on November 18, 1981 that the first solid mention of the completion of my court settlement is documented. My case manager notes that I had finished my court settlement, and within the next six months, I would be moving toward my goal of opening my own kennel. This is the only place this it is mentioned in my ALTA files.

The ALTA files then mention that I had developed a staph infection in my forehead. I would need major surgery. The quarterly progress report notes as follows:

That on May 5, 1982, I would have the first surgery to remove a bone flap in the front of my forehead at Doctor's Hospital. Then, six months recuperation period in Cameron Park near Sacramento. Then, a second surgery approximately mid-September in order to place a plate in my forehead. I would be moving out of the Parks Residential Facility effective May 5, 1982 and would not be in the area or have any sort of program plan or activities until March or April of 1983 some ten months later.

In the documents I have from ALTA, there is a referral that in 1981 there was no "movement toward legalized conservatorship at this time." However, on April 2, 1982, my mother informed my caseworker, Elizabeth Oakes, that my "father" was now my legal conservator. This meant he had complete control over my life, rights, and money. My caseworker asked my mother to send her copies of the papers for my ALTA file. It is interesting to note there are no copies of those papers. Nor in all the ALTA files from all the years he was my conservator is there any place where the conservatorship paperwork actually appears. I have never seen any actual legal documentation of the start of my conservatorship, although I am quite curious about it. I wonder what it really does say in those papers, and as I write this, I am still working on trying to find the documentation about it. (*Note*: January 2006—In the past few months, we finally got copies of my old court records, and the information about my conservatorship has come to light. It will be covered later on as we go along.)

As for myself, I don't have any memory of any of that happening. I don't remember them telling me that Lou was now my conservator or the implications of what that meant. It's possible that they might have told me about it and I simply don't remember. It wouldn't have mattered to me anyways if they had. It would be years before I came to understand what it all meant and how it would impact my life, and then, it would become a very, very big deal!

The next notation in my file says that my caseworker visited me at Doctor's Medical Center on Monday May 10, 1982 after my surgery. She writes that I was alert and appeared to have no ill effect from having the bone flap removed. The plans were that I would still spend most of my recuperation time up in Placerville with a family friend. She notes that I would be coming back to Modesto to live after my next surgery. My mother asked her to keep my file open because of that. The last note from Elizabeth Oaks in my file is a little over four months later on September 21, 1982. She notes that Cindy Kenley from ALTA Regional Center in Placerville had called her to tell her that my family had moved to the Placerville area and was contacting ALTA for socialization services for me and that ALTA was asking for a transfer of my file.

Chapter 4

We move to El Dorado County
(I finally get to move toward independence)

When I first went to El Dorado County, I was staying with a family friend while I was recovering from the surgery on the bone flap in my skull.

It was after that that I slowly became aware that there had been some sort of significant financial settlement as a result of my accident. In researching what the amounts were, I have found that the man who hit me with the truck had a business that was hired by the city of Modesto. I was never told of the specific amounts of the settlement that I can remember. Only that I gathered it was fairly large. After my accident, while I struggled to live and regain some small part of myself, I was completely unaware of the legal battle that had been going on.

In February, about six months after my accident, we signed the paperwork for Lou to become my guardian. This gave him the ability to represent me in court and sign legal paperwork for me. I was still a minor, but this was the legal avenue that was needed to get things started.

In February of '79, Lou had his attorney file a complaint for damages against the man who was driving the '76 Ford truck, his brother (as copartner in the company) and the company that he worked for. This was settled for $50,000 in June of '79, just under a year from the time of my accident. This was then divided into thirds. It was supposed to be divided into equal thirds: one third to Blue Shield (for the lien in excess of $80,000), one third to the attorneys, and one third to me. So, out of the $50,000, I would have ended up with $16,639. Interestingly enough, when I got the actual court documents, the judge had changed the amounts so that I actually got $18,277.

There was then the city of Modesto to contend with, as the man had been doing duties for the city when I was hit.

In August of '79, a year after my accident, paperwork was filed to bring my case against the city of Modesto. The legal documents say that my injury was severe and would have a devastating impact on my life permanently. This has proved to be quite true. The attorneys said that I would continue to suffer pain and mental anguish for a long period of time, and that as a result of said injuries, I had been "generally damaged" in a sum in excess of the "jurisdictional limits" of the Municipal Court.

In other words, the injuries I sustained were so bad that my case needed to be heard by the Stanislaus Supreme Court, and a "cause of action" was filed for it to be moved there. The final settlement with the city of Modesto is dated November 13, 1981. It took approximately a year and nine months to be settled. And reads as such: That there would be a $225,000 up-front cash settlement; $5,384,066 representing periodic payments of $1,500 per month for the span of my lifetime, increasing at 6 percent per year; and $300,000 for attorney's fees. There were also medical liens and a Medi-Cal bill to be paid, which totaled up to about $56,000. That was paid out of the cash settlement to me. I never knew any of this until spring of 2005. Funny that for all these years, I have been receiving the money but was never told any of the specifics of it that I remember.

I was now living with our family friend in El Dorado County and recovering from my surgery. I would ride my bike along the country roads there (I now always wore a helmet). I found I liked the area, and according to my family, I found the Greenstone property and wanted my family to buy it as the place to run the animal kennel we had discussed before my surgery, and they did. This is when I first really became aware of the settlement and its connection to me. From what I can remember, I found the ranch and then my parents bought it, and I lived with the family friend in the house for a while, then she wanted more money to take care of me, and she left and my parents then moved in with me. I would be willing to guess that Lou wasn't paying her very much, and from what I have read (because I don't remember), I must have been quite a handful to look after twenty-four hours a day. I don't wonder that she wanted more, and I can guess that Lou wasn't inclined to pay what it was worth to her. I am not sure how my living there with her ties into the kennel because she and I certainly didn't have one while she was there. But then when she left and my family moved in, that seems to be when the kennel business was "supposed" to happen. Which was really something of a joke as you will see.

Lou came up with the name "The Very Important Pet Motel," which I thought was pretty good. Since I had planned to be a veterinarian and could not now be one, we instead would board animals and I would help take care of them. The reality turned out to be quite another thing. Once they moved in, things started to change. They purchased items that had nothing to do with me, as far as I could tell. In fact, they bought horses (and a truck and horse trailer) I could not ride, because I couldn't take the risk of falling off and hurting myself again. A ski boat that I couldn't use, because (again) of the limitation of my hand and not being able to take the chance of further injury. I have searched my mind and have no memories of being in the boat. I'm not saying I wasn't, because I can't be 100 percent sure, just that I have no memory of it and I really don't think I was.

I certainly didn't mind that they bought these things, but I later learned that they were listed in the inventory of "my" assets, meaning they bought them with my money for my use. I didn't realize at the time that they had bought the boat with my money. If I had, I would have been more than slightly displeased. It wouldn't have been my choice as to how to spend my money; at least I don't think so, looking back at it. I thought that I remembered that they took vacations that I never got to go on. My mother disputes this and says I couldn't be left alone, so perhaps I am wrong. With my mother's "faulty" memory, however, it's hard for me to know what to believe with regards to her. From my perspective, it felt like they took over when they moved in. As I became aware of what was happening, this made me very angry because I knew I had paid for some of the price of the house, and I expected that that would give me some sort of say in it, but it did not. I had been essentially living independently while living in the care homes, but now, I was back under my parents' control and what they considered to be "their roof." Although I knew I had paid for at least some of that roof!

In retrospect, I can see that in those early days, they tried to do things to give me the life that I wanted. I don't know why the kennel didn't work out, but it didn't. I'm guessing that neither Louis nor my mother really wanted to run a kennel and it would take a lot of supervision for me to be able to. As well as I don't think we were getting along very well from the time they moved in and took control of the house.

I don't ever remember having any animals boarded there at all. They also had a pool put in, but it wasn't done right and it had to have a new liner put in six months after the pool was installed, which then cost more of my money (I didn't realize that this was also my money at the time). I do think that they bought the land for a good investment, and it did become worth more as time went by. I can say that from this time on, I was aware of the money and that Lou was in charge of it. And that made me angry because I didn't feel like I was getting a fair cut of my own money, even back then when I lived at home. The feeling only got worse as time went by. And again, I was aware that I had paid for a chunk of the house, and yet, getting no say in how I lived there.

The other thing that seemed to begin happening then that I recall the most, was that Lou started telling me everyday that I was going to die. He didn't do it with love or compassion or ask me to change the way I did things. He got to the point where he *insisted* that I was going to die. This filled me with rage, and it was as if he was pushing me into it on purpose. Day after day he would tell me this. I realized at that time that Lou now finally had my mother also completely under his control and that greed had gotten the best of them. And I couldn't speak to rebut them or even stand up for myself. My feelings were that once Lou got control of my money and greed corrupted him, and if I was dead, he could do whatever he wanted with my money and not have to account to anyone for it.

What I was unaware of at the time was that my family had turned the property and the "business" into a corporation (of the Very Important Pet Motel) and that they had put all of my assets into the "corporation," including the ranch property itself. My stepdad was the president, my mother the VP, and my older sister Stephanie the treasurer. This meant that if something had happened to me, all of my assets belonged to the corporation and not to me any longer, so there wouldn't even have been inheritance tax. Pretty sneaky, huh? I never knew this till recent years when I got the court papers from Stanislaus County where they talk about the probation department discovering all this, but I'll go into the exact details of that in later chapters. I did know that something was going on at the time that wasn't right; I just didn't know what it was.

Following the notes in my ALTA file, I see that Cindy Kenley contacted Elizabeth Oaks for info about me in the fall of 1982. Then made a home visit on December 10, 1982. It says that I expressed a desire to meet other people near my age. Cindy mentions MORE Workshop as a place that might be good for me. Cindy also mentions to my mother about different family support groups for us to go to. On January 5, 1983, Cindy logs a phone call from my mother indicating that she and I were interested in an out-of-home placement for me. It says that I was feeling the need to exert more independence and would like to be in a more independent living situation than living in my family's home. Again, the fact of the matter was that in reality, my parents had comingled their funds with mine (from my court settlement, my 65 percent to their 35 percent). So in a way, it was more my house then theirs. But I was not really aware that it was more my house then theirs at that time. I wouldn't have known what that meant anyway. On March 21, 1983, Cindy made another home visit and discussed placement options with my parents and me. I was interested in a semi-independent living arrangement that would gear me toward a more independent living facility. Cindy notes that she would attend a placement committee meeting the beginning of April in order to arrange it.

In March of '83, I began attending the MORE workshop. They came up with a plan to help me develop more skills, especially my manual dexterity and communication skills. I was working on the "baler" and the book cover machine. It's noted that when I would get angry or frustrated, I would walk out of the building, which is quite a bit of advancement from how I used to be. I was told, however, that I wouldn't be paid for the time that I left the production area. They wanted me to go to a staff member when I was angry and try to work it out. They did feel that my leaving the work area was an appropriate measure for me at that time. My main goals at this time were to make money in the workshop area and to increase some academic skills.

My own personal perceptions of the time are still fuzzy, but in general I liked the workshop and the people. Most of them are still dear friends to me now, and my family and I enjoy visiting them.

April of 1983 is when we started discussing the cluster apartments in Davis through Summer House. My parents said the kennel wasn't working out, and I was ready to get away. From what I remember, there wasn't anything to work out. We never boarded any animals that I remember at all. I was tired of living with my parents, however, and went for a visit to Summer House and really liked it. I liked both the apartments and the vocational situation there at UC Davis in the food service program. I went for a three-hour trial at the cafeteria and enjoyed it very much. I scrubbed pots and pans. It was easy work and I knew what I was doing, which also made me feel better about myself. There was little stress in that sort of job.

There was a slight delay while I had surgery to have a skull plate put in my forehead.

I moved in to the cluster apartments three months later on July 1, 1983. I had some difficulties communicating with my roommates, however. It is written in my files (because I still don't remember this time in my life well) that they also had communication difficulties, but the staff there was determined to help us get through it. At this time, my ALTA case was transferred from the Placerville ALTA to the Woodland ALTA. My new counselor, Jesse Otero, came to see me in October of '83. I was doing very well then in both the cluster and the cafeteria. The next ALTA note is in June of '84, eight months later. It says I had been in the program for a year then and that I would need another year of service there. It says also that my goals were to work as a kitchen worker in unsubsidized competitive employment. It says that I had a goal of learning to deal more effectively with my own limitations by becoming more independent in problem solving and adapting to changes in my work environment in an appropriate, professional manner without becoming impatient or verbally abusive.

Something that was very important to me I want to mention here. Shortly after I moved to Davis, I was able to accomplish something I had wanted to do again since my accident, and that was to ride my unicycle again. I had thought about it a lot since my accident, and to me, it represented getting back to a previous state of "normality." I had been able to ride the unicycle before my accident, and it was one of my long-standing goals to be able to do it again. During the time I was in the wheelchair, I kept thinking about wanting to be able to ride the unicycle, and it made me both sad and angry that I couldn't do it anymore. So, being able to ride again was a big success for me. This was sort of a proof to me that I was back on my feet again and closer to who I had been before the accident.

Looking back on it, I must have been a real challenge to work with. I did not have much patience then, and even now, it's something I have to work on. Again, I didn't mean to be challenging, I just was. It was, after all, only five years after having had my brains scrambled pretty good, and on the traumatic brain injury timeline, that's not much time.

In November of '84, a special meeting was held to discuss my present and future situation. Another six months of the "satellite" program was requested. I had graduated from the cluster apartments by then and was living more independently. I also had been independent in my work for the past six months and was not receiving support services from the Department of Rehabilitation anymore. In July of '85, I was dropped down to only fifteen hours of maintenance level Independent Living Skills services (from the fifty I had started with when I first moved into the Summer House program). I had another annual review in November of '85 and was dropped to seven hours of support services.

The next note in my file is not until almost a year later, on October 29, 1986. I'd had a couple of different ALTA caseworkers by then, and my counselor was now Jan Lee. My file says that my counselor talked with my mother, who said she was very pleased with the services which I had been receiving. Mother told my counselor that I had recently been home for my birthday celebration and that I appeared to be happier and more relaxed than the family had ever seen me since my accident. It also notes that because Lou was my conservator, that copies of my report would be sent to him.

I was still working in the cafeteria, and Lou was only sending me $500 in addition to what I made from work, which I think was about $75 every two weeks, so it wasn't much to live on. I do know that I thought about the fact that Lou had all my money (even though I didn't know how much it was at the time) and was living on that big ranch and that I was just scraping by on about $650 a month. This upset me considerably, and I know I thought about it twenty-four hours a day. My mother notes in the above paragraph that I was "happy and relaxed." This was to some degree a front I was putting on so that Lou would leave me alone and not disrupt my life as it was. I was mostly independent, and I didn't want him to change it. My memory is that he had threatened to lock me up if I didn't behave, so I never ever confronted him on my money situation and just pretended that everything was hunky-dory, when in fact, I was very upset about the situation. But there was nothing that I could do about it at the time. I was very scared to lose the independence I was gaining. You will see later in a letter from Lou himself that he did threaten to "lock me up" if I didn't behave, and said the courts would demand that he do this. That was not really the case; the courts never intended to lock me up. It was just a threat that Lou used to keep me in line. It worked. (Later when my mother reviewed this part of the manuscript, she underlined the part about it working and added several exclamation marks to indicate that Lou's way of handling me had been a good thing! We still disagree on that.)

In November of '86, my annual IPP meeting was held again, and this time all purchased services were discontinued. I was doing very well on my own and did not need their assistance anymore. I thanked the staff for all of their help over the past couple of years. Lon Springer (the Director of Summer House) and I had become good friends, and he volunteered to keep in touch with me on a friendly basis. I also discontinued Vocational Training Services at my work, as I didn't need that anymore either. I felt that I had settled into my new life very well by now. I had been living and working in Davis for four years and mostly enjoyed my life. It was also during this time that I was having more trouble breathing. I had had problems since my accident, but it seemed to be getting worse as I got older. Then it became like I was breathing underwater all the time. This made me more aggravated and frustrated, and harder for me to concentrate on things.

The next section gets a bit rocky. After four years of relative stability and progress and living my own life, things were about to change.

Chapter 5

The Dark Ages
(I suffer some setbacks and Lou is investigated)

While in Davis (as I have stated previously), I worked at the cafeteria, and that is where I had most of my meals. I worked washing pots and pans. I had been doing very well living independently. On April 6, 1987, my friend Lon called my caseworker to tell her that I had resigned my job because I was unhappy with my new supervisor and I was feeling it was time to change jobs. Lon said that he intended to help me look for another job and also requested (on my behalf) that rehabilitation resume services with me. Lon also expressed frustration as to how to best help me. Lon wondered if a current evaluation of my skills and deficits and learning abilities could be completed. My counselor notes that she would consult with the ALTA staff psychologists regarding this. My ALTA caseworker then notes that she is working on compiling past testing and preparing to have new testing done. During this time, I went into a severe depression. This was because of my breathing problems.

Unknown to me at the time, there were some legal difficulties brewing simultaneously for Lou. In June of '87, the court investigator for Stanislaus County asked for a continuance to complete her report and review the accounting of my estate that Lou had filed. She further requested that he make himself available to discuss the accounting with her.

At this time, two things began happening almost concurrently. My ALTA files say that on July 16, 1987 (a month later), my friend Lon called and told my ALTA caseworker that my parents had moved me from my apartment in Davis back home to Greenstone with them. In looking at the recently acquired legal documents from El Dorado County, this is the exact month that the Stanislaus County conservatorship investigator began seriously investigating Lou for mishandling my money. Coincidence? I don't think so!

On August 17, 1987, Cindy Kenley told Jan Lee (my caseworker in Woodland) that my mother had called Cindy Kenley at the Placerville ALTA to say she was interested in some social and recreational activities for me. My mother also told Cindy that I did not wish to receive any ALTA services of any kind at that time. I don't believe that I was aware enough of what was going on at the time to make that sort of decision, so it is my feeling now that they wanted to keep me isolated from people that might help me. I then seem to disappear from the bureaucratic radar for approximately nineteen months. My file at ALTA was inactivated on November 12, 1987 with the note that "the Presleys were no longer interested in any service that ALTA might provide." We find this quite interesting, considering the fact that almost ever since my accident, my mother had worked hard to utilize all of the ALTA programs that she could. But now, I was not to be involved with any of them. It was very true that my breathing problem had gotten so severe that I could hardly breathe or think, and that I really didn't care about anything at the time but getting it fixed. From what I remember, it was fairly shortly after I came home that they had my nose fixed so I could breathe better than I ever had since my accident.

In September, the court disapproved the accounting in its present form. In October, Lou's attorney filed an amended petition for settlement of the third accounting and report of conservator.

On December 2, 1987, the court ordered that the public defender be appointed to represent me in this. The reason for this is that the court investigator had found many discrepancies in the accounting that Lou had filed. She was also concerned about the fact that he sent me so little money to live on and from what she could see no extra spending money. There were also grave concerns about the Very Important Pet Motel and the fact that my father had loaned all of my extra savings to it. As well as the fact that the Greenstone property was **not** in my name (as it should have been legally), but in that of the VIP Motel. The corporate papers listed my mother, Lou, and my older sister Stephanie as the corporate board members and stockholders. All in all, the public defender lists some thirteen different "irregularities" within the last accounting of my estate at this time.

I had no idea at the time that there were any legal difficulties going on, so they hid it from me very well. I think that because of his mishandling my money, they needed me to be living on the premises to stay out of trouble.

There was quite a bit of back-and-forth between the public defender, the court investigator, Lou, his attorneys, and the court. Lou was temporarily removed as my conservator of the estate, pending resolution of the matter, but he was allowed to remain conservator of the person.

The accounting was disapproved twice before it was finally done to the satisfaction of the court. Lou came very close to being permanently removed as my conservator at the time, and he had to do some quick backpedaling to hang on to my estate.

There is a response from Lou to the court as to why things were as they were. In the disapproved accounting, the DA states that one of her concerns was that I was not provided an allowance or any other monies over and above my rent expenses. In Lou's reply to the court, he states that he called my caseworker at ALTA and asked them how much of my monies I should receive. According to him, he was simply going along with what they said he should pay.

We should note here that we have read all through the ALTA files and the caseworkers were very conscientious at logging all phone conversations and other interactions with my parents. The conversation that Lou refers to does not appear in any of the ALTA documentation that we have. As an aside, we had a long speakerphone conversation with my ALTA caseworker about this recently to ask her how she would handle such a request, and her answer was that if someone had an existing payee, then ALTA would never give any dollar amount recommendation and that ALTA did not give advice to clients' payees on how to handle their money situations. She also said specifically that if such a conversation had taken place, it would be well-documented in the files.

Of course we realize that my current caseworker is not the one that Lou would have talked to, but it would seem that the answer would be pretty much the same.

The court ordered him to sell the property and dissolve the VIP Motel Corporation, as it was all done illegally according to the conservator statutes. One of the main reasons they had to sell the property was that they had comingled their money with mine—a huge no-no as far as conservatorship rules go.

It is evident that Lou was playing a sneaky game with my money, no matter what noble thoughts my family may have about it. Looking through the paperwork, it's no wonder that the VIP Motel made no money, as there was never any advertising done until the court began investigating the corporation. The advertising budget appears to have been a total of $64 for all of '85, '86, and '87. It was a grand total of four ads. Again, interestingly enough, the advertising budget was in June and July of 1987, the very time that the court was investigating Lou. In those three years, $91,268 was spent on the "business." $6,912 was paid by my parents, leaving the fact that in the three years covered by the third accounting, $84,355 of *my* money was spent at the Very Important Pet Motel, and yet, it made ***not one penny***. In fact, in all the years the business existed, it made not one penny. Hence, my perception that we never boarded any pets is shown to be accurate. Lou was also reprimanded by the court for comingling his money with mine. This is strictly against the laws governing conservatorships.

My personal feeling was that the reason all of this was put into the VIP Motel, was that my stepfather kept saying I was going to die, and if I did, since none of this was in my name, there would be no estate taxes or issues to handle as it all belonged to the corporation, not to me. This was the very thing that he was reprimanded for by the DA. It felt to me like in a way he was trying to program me to die, but I did not. I was Mr. Determination, and I was determined to live and somehow achieve the life I dreamt of.

Later, when Lou sold the Greenstone property (by floating the loan which was later defaulted on and the home nearly destroyed), he then bought another house which was in Lodi and, breaking the laws of conservatorships, comingled my money with his, yet ***again***! There were no repercussions for his breaking the conservatorship laws yet again, and yet again it proves that he did not obey the laws and was not the honest up-front person that my sister and mother say that he was.

In one of the latter court documents, Lou states that both times he did follow the proper procedures and petitioned the court to be allowed to comingle the funds and also to buy the properties. We have read and reread the court documents from the time of my accident to the time my conservatorship changed through to its dismissal in latter years, and nowhere are there any documents submitted to the court asking for permission to either comingle or to buy the properties themselves. Nor are there any asking for an assessment of the properties as is part of the court procedure for conservators before buying properties. They are also required to have a court "referee" give an assessment of a properties value before it is sold, and we could not find any of those either. This comes into play when in latter years Lou would sell one of the acquired properties at a loss. We have asked the court clerk that if those papers were submitted to the court, is there any place else they might be, and her response was that all documents are in chronological order, and that any requests made to the court and response from the court would be in the files we were looking at, and if the papers had been submitted to the court, they would be there. She was very black-and-white about it. As there is a flurry of papers to and from the court when such a request is made, then it would not be a matter of "a" document missing, but for all the documents would have to be missing. So we can only surmise by the fact that those documents are not there, that in fact, Lou never did ask the court's permission to either comingle the monies, or to buy or sell either of the two properties that he acquired and sold during his time as my conservator.

However, we did see those same sorts of documented requests to buy property twice to the court from my new conservator, Bill Cody, there in the records. So I wonder: if Lou did it twice, why was neither there?

I never lived in nor saw the Lodi house until years later. Although my parents stated that I had always had a bedroom there. Interesting, as I never set foot in it nor would I have been welcome. I know this because they had refused to visit me when I was living in my own apartment off of Cold Springs Road. They told Romana that they were afraid if they came to visit, that I would want to move home with them. Well, if I had a room in the house that they spent my money on, what would have been wrong with that? This is exactly the kind of thing that needs to be changed in the conservatorship laws and should have been a perfect reason to replace Lou as my conservator at that time without having to spend my money to fight him for years! That, along with the fact that he had already been reprimanded for mishandling my money and yet there was no disciplinary action when he turned around and bought another house and comingled the funds again without the courts permission. No wonder he thought he could get away with whatever he wanted, because for the most part, he could!

A point brought up by my attorney, Bruce Kimzy, is that they were living in a house that I owned most of, but they never paid any rent to me.

The bottom line is that he was **not** following the law, and repeatedly, he and my family were taking advantage of me. And again, it was during this time that I had no interaction with ALTA or anyone else outside my family that I can remember.

This is a good time for me to bring up more about this breathing problem. It should be noted that since my accident, I had a very difficult time breathing. Everyone thought it was allergies, and I was always getting shots that only helped a tiny bit. At last, a surgery on my nasal passages was done, and I was amazed that I could finally breathe clearly again, like I had before my accident. It had been about fifteen years of additional suffering. Now I could finally breathe and eat at the same time.

In polite society, we are taught to eat with our mouths closed. But I had to eat with mine open so I could breathe. I would hide my mouth with my hand and be very embarrassed and aware that it seemed I had no eating manners, when in fact, I was mortified at how I had to eat. Because of that, I tried to avoid eating around other people when I could. I did not want people to think I was some sort of troll with no manners. I did that for roughly nine years. Not being able to breathe had contributed a lot to my short temper. After the surgery, I thanked God, and I feel it was then that my attitude started to get better. It also seemed like I could think clearer and I wasn't always concerned about how difficult my next breath would be. My breathing problem had also made me feel suicidal sometimes because it was extremely frustrating to be feeling like I was breathing underwater all the time. I couldn't focus on anything, and it's amazing that I got as far as I did the way things had been. I remember waking up after the nasal surgery and feeling like I had just gotten a new lease on life. And now I could eat normally too!

I don't really know what happened to me from July of '87 until January of '89 (about nineteen months) when my case was reopened at the ALTA in Placerville. That reactivation file, opened by Jane Williamson, notes that my parents said I had made some "bad decisions," but they refused to give any examples except for my falling off my bike and getting hurt once. Jane then notes that she spoke with both my friend Lon and my ex ALTA caseworker, and they both concurred that I had a "minimal" of bad experiences while in Davis. My breathing problem was the only thing I cared about at that moment. Once that was fixed, I felt like life was worth getting involved with again.

One of the things I remember most about that time was mowing the lawns for what seemed like hours and wanting to get away from Lou. Back and forth, back and forth I went, getting madder by the minute. It seemed like there was nothing else to think of at the time. I had to pretend that everything was fine when it wasn't. I was furious inside, and now that my nose was fixed, I just wanted to leave as fast as I could. I was remembering how independent I had been in Davis, and now here I was, trapped, back in Greenstone, living with my parents—*again*. It felt like a prison to me. I was also angry about how much I didn't know about my money situation, and I was terrified to ask Lou and rock the boat. I was angry and frustrated that I couldn't speak to ask Lou the questions that I wanted to about my money. It was another catch-22. I was angry because I couldn't ask about the money since I was afraid of the reaction if I did, and they wouldn't volunteer the information or speak to me about it of their own accord, so I had no answers about my financial information. I very much wanted to know how much money I had, but I was terrified to ask and make Lou mad. I was afraid he would yell at me as he did about other things all the time. Lou had a very bad temper. It took a while to get him mad, but when he did, he was very ugly. He was one of those people who hated to be questioned about anything. He took it as a personal insult, and believe me, you didn't want to be on the receiving end of that if you could help it. So I just swallowed my fury and existed as best I could, pretending to smile and be happy, but I wasn't. And I always wondered about my money and how much I had and what he was doing with it. It was then that I really began to resent and hate him more and more.

I had the distinct feeling that I was being taken advantage of, but I just didn't know how much. I didn't know if it was a lot or a little, but I had a feeling it was a pretty good amount. All this spun around in my head while I mowed. The more I mowed, the madder I got. When you're mowing for what seems like hour after hour, you have time not just to think about these things, but obsess about every little detail of them as well. I had grass allergies also, but I took medication for it and that helped. I thought about all this twenty-four hours a day at the time, so it wasn't just while I was mowing. But the mowing seemed to focus it more at the time.

On February 6, 1989, there is a note from my caseworker, Jane Williamson, reactivating my file at ALTA. I met her at her office there, and my parents spoke with her on the phone. Then on April 7, 1989, there was a meeting at MORE workshop. I had had an evaluation done there, and it had gone very well. I began working there again. It felt wonderful to be back there with some of my longtime friends. They greeted me like I had never been away. After the isolation of the past year and a half, it was great to be away from my parents, even just for those few hours a day. The next note from Jane a few days later says that I met all of my goals in one week. New goals were established that focused on my teaching to others the use of the paper-shredding equipment and operating the book-cutting machine.

I was thrilled to be back at MORE and out of the house with some time away from my parents, mostly Lou. I remember being very anxious to move out on my own again at the time.

Some fifteen months later on 7/2/90, Jane logs a call from my mother saying that I would be spending the weekend at Pathways (a group home for developmentally disabled adults) from 7/6/90 to 7/8/90.

On 7/9/90, Susie Davies called Jane at ALTA to tell her that I had had a "wonderful weekend at Pathways" and that I would be moving in there on 8/2/90.

On 8/2/90, I moved into Pathways. At first, I enjoyed it, but after a while it began to feel like a prison because I had to go everywhere with the group whether I wanted to or not, and I desired a more independent life like the one I'd had in Davis. I had a goal to move out and live independently again. I was aware that some of the folks at Pathways had severe disabilities, and I was concerned that when I was seen in public with them, that people would think I was like them. Not that I thought I was better than them, but I was very different from them. I had different goals in my life than they, and now I was not going to be able to live the life I had grown up thinking I would. To me, it was like having grown up with a life in color, and now it felt like it was in black and white. I knew what I could no longer do. I found this enraging. Because I could not talk, I could not tell people my story. When we were in public, I often tried to separate myself from them by being ahead of them, or way behind them. But the staff would get mad at me and tell me I had to stay with the group. This was the *last* thing I wanted to do.

On 2/21/91, there is a note from my new caseworker, Stacy Lee, which said that I expressed my desire to live on my own. My parents said, however, that they wanted me to wait until my next birthday (in October some eight months later) to discuss the issue further.

In addition to my living situation, I was now working two jobs. In the morning, I worked as a supply clerk and janitor at Super Plumbing. I started working there in October of 1990. I really liked it there. The boss, Vince Panto, was an outstanding guy who took me under his wing and gave me lots of support. The employees and I had many outings as a group. We went rafting and camping, and I loved the people there. I can't say enough good things about them still.

In the afternoons, I worked at MORE workshop. This was my second round there. My specialty was the shredder. There were not many people that they let work the shredder. I did cut myself one time on it and bled a lot and I needed some stitches, then I had to go through some additional safety training. I still have the scar to show. I made many friends while at MORE and am still dear friends with Vince and Susie Davies, who is now (as I write this) the executive director of MORE. We get together for lunch or dinner roughly every couple of months. As I write this now, after years of hardships induced by my parents, I have come to the conclusion that Susie and Vince are the best working role models that I have ever had. They never belittled me, but they did tell me things straight out even when I disagreed with them. And I thank them for everything that they have done for me, especially in the times before I learned to control my temper outbursts. I know I had been challenging sometimes, but they always had patience with me, and I will always love them deeply for that.

I have a letter from Lou, dated February 7, 1991. I guess this is about the time that we started discussing my moving out on my own.

February 7, 1991

Dear Todd:

I understand you are pushing to live on your own again. One important thing you don't seem to understand or even try to understand is that your living on your own is controlled by the Court. You must prove by your behavior, your ability to take care of your own needs before you can live on your own. The fact that you are still having temper tantrums and bullying women and generally behaving like a person who intends to hurt other people will not cut it. Also you are now on your own as to taking your pills and the evidence is that you do not seem able to do that since pills are found on the floor around the place. It may be that your general bad temper might be caused by your failure to take your pills properly. When you were in Davis you were not taking proper care of yourself and the people who were there to help you were constantly frustrated because you ran them off and refused to listen to their attempts to help you. (they were also female. Do you get the picture?) The truth is that you somehow think you are Mr. know-it-all and you don't or won't realize how very limited you are in handling your own affairs.

If and when you're finally are living (on your own) in Placerville you will again have people around to help you and if you treat them the same as you treat everyone else who wants to help you, NOT control you, the only answer the court will come up with is to place you in a locked facility. You simply must learn to act in a civilized manner if you are ever going to live the way you seem to want to.

In order for you to be able to live somewhere else by April first would require a court study, all kinds of evaluations, a whole lot of help from us and that is absurd. In the first place the court must be made aware of it and approve and from your recent actions you can bet odds on that they will not permit it.

The program you are in now is the best you will ever have and they seem to be helping you and somehow that I don't understand they seem to really care for you. Why are you in such a hurry to leave them? Why don't you act more like a real gentleman instead of being such a jerk.

Somewhere around your birthday the court will be sending someone to interview you to see how you live and how you are getting along with people. I would like to suggest that you get your act together. Stop being stupid and let someone see to it that you take your pills. You had better control your temper. Be cooperative. Try to understand your limitations so that when the court investigator does show up they would have a picture they could approve. They were certainly mad about your situation in Davis and forced us to bring you home. If you live on your own and they again see a similar situation to Davis they will demand you be brought home or placed in a locked facility.

Shape up, Todd. Stop being a jerk. You were not taught that way.

Dad

You can see from the text of the letter what Lou thought of me at the time. Others have told me that they were aghast at some of Lou's behaviors. In the meeting where we talked about my living independently, he said that what I really needed was a "little Asian woman to look after me." Susie was not at the meeting, but was told about the incident. She is of Asian background, and this did not go over very well with her. I was personally mortified that he said such a thing. I might have had my problems, but I was never a bigot.

It was with Stacy's determination and support that I was able to overcome my parents' objections to my desire to live independently again. I was signed up to work with an agency called Choices Transitional Services. They provided independent living skills training. This would prove to be my greatest path to freedom.

Chapter 6

And They said I Couldn't Do It
(Leaving the group home and moving
into my second apartment)

I was working at a place called Super Plumbing in the mornings doing stocking of plumbing supplies in the warehouse and straitening things up outside. I became very close friends with the owner, Vince Panto, and the other employees there. They really mentored me and went out of their way to help me with work and to include me in many of their outside activities as well. They gave me a male bonding experience I'd never had to that level before. To be so included in the group was wonderful. It was truly some of the happiest times I'd ever had to that point. And I felt the most accepted that I ever had by "normal" people since my accident. We would go for rides and camping and white-water rafting. They were my buddies and made my life very happy and count for more than just living in the group home. They had a lot of patience with me and went out of their way to help me. It was the first time in my life that I had "normal" guy friends to do "normal" guy stuff with. They all made me feel a part of the Super Plumbing family, and they made it one of the happier times in my life. I am still very close with Vince, although he has retired and Super Plumbing no longer exists. My family and I see him and his family along with Susie every couple of months. I cherish his friendship dearly.

I would like to take a moment to encourage others to do the same for the less-abled who may be among you. Especially if they are like I was, and locked up in a group home. You have no idea how important this sort friendship can be. If you were to ever want to do something to reach out, this is a perfect way to do it. Many of the disabled now work simple jobs in the community. I am sure that the vast majority of them would cherish this sort of friendship, and you will find that they can give as much back to you as you can to them. Just give them a chance. Ask them out for pizza or to go to the movies or something like that. You will find you too can change a life, just like Vince and his employees changed mine, and make lifelong friends! The power of joy that simple act can bring is amazing to the person. Of course, not everyone will be like that, but I'd be more than willing to bet that most of them will enjoy it very much. This is a simple way to "pay it forward."

So, I worked at Super Plumbing in the mornings, then in the afternoon, I would walk the half mile to MORE workshop and work there in the afternoons.

I had been living at Pathways for seven months now.

My new ILS instructor came to meet me there. Her name was Romana. That was March 1, 1991. First, I had to have what's called an "assessment," which was a variety of tests of my independent living skills to see what I would need to learn to be able to live independently. This was stuff like making my bed, cooking simple meals, simple budgets, laundry skills, social skills, and traffic-and-health awareness. This gave an overall view of where I was at the time. Which I was told was pretty high. I had a few things I needed to work on though.

We discussed where I wanted to live, and I told Romana that I wanted to be able to walk to both jobs. I wanted to be able to shop at the Raley's on Placerville Drive. This was one reason I had been embarrassed when out with the other clients from Pathways. I knew I would be on my own soon and not be able to explain my situation to those in the community who had seen me with them.

We had amazing luck. The very first apartment I went to look at was in a perfect location for me, less then a half mile to Super Plumbing, just a bit over that to MORE and three quarters of a mile to the store. I filled out the application and got the apartment. I thanked God, both for finding it and that things went so smoothly in getting it.

We then went shopping for furniture. I knew I wanted the black leather La-Z-Boy sofas from Levitz. I have seen the commercials on TV for years and years, and I knew that was what I wanted when I had my own home again. We went to Levitz twice, the first time to price the furniture, and the second to buy it and arrange delivery. Lou didn't give me any problems at this point about what I wanted and for that I was grateful. I had high hopes that all would go well now that I could breathe freely and that I would now be independent and have my own home once more after so long a delay. It had been four years since I had had my own place, and now at last, I had it again.

It was a wonderful day when it was all delivered and set up. It was not easy at first, but with a lot of support, I not only succeeded, I thrived. Although I invited my parents many times to come visit me, they declined, saying they had trips to take or other things they needed to do.

After many phone calls and invitations that were refused, Romana finally pinned my mother down to an answer as to the reason they wouldn't visit me. My mother told Romana that she was afraid that if they came to visit me, I would want to move home with them. *Not!* What thirty-year-old wants to willingly live with his parents? I had already lived on my own for several years while in Davis, and I loved living on my own. I would not have gone back to live with my parents after Davis if it hadn't been for my depression and frustration because of my breathing problem. I just wanted to show them how well I was doing now. It was during this time that my mother told Romana that after my accident, since I was so different, that they had talked about doing a "renaming" ceremony for me. I wanted nothing to do with this, and I felt hurt, insulted, and angry by it. I think most of this came from Lou who was a conservative Jew. We are dealing with a specific individual and how *he* interpreted things. I doubt that most other people would have felt this way about the situation, which I believe was this:

My family was told that I was going to die, but I didn't. However, I was a greatly changed person after this, and because I couldn't say the Jewish prayers anymore, to Lou it was almost as if I was dead. I think that is why they wanted to rename me, because they felt I was not the person that I had been. My feelings go like this: That Lou thought that because I couldn't talk and say prayers, it was like I was mostly dead. Therefore, since I was mostly dead, I wasn't really a person. So, he could discount me and use my money as he saw fit, regardless of how that affected me. I, however, felt very much alive, especially when very frustrated. I feel that my mom didn't really agree with Lou on this but had no choice but to go along if she didn't want to rock her family boat too much. I was mad at her at the time for not standing up for me, but now I understand her position much better, and I have forgiven her for those times. In retrospect and all fairness to her, I think she was living as much under Lou's thumb as I was. Romana would try to point this out to me, but I felt at the time that as my mother, she should have stood up for me regardless of her situation. There were a couple of times I threatened to throw Romana out if she continued to insist that my mother was doing the best she could. But I have since come to understand much more that Romana was right about the situation that my mother was in at the time. However, now Romana doesn't feel that she was right. Because at this point and time, Lou has been gone for several years, and my mother still maintains that Lou was upstanding and right in how he handled me and my money. Romana always thought that once Lou was gone, my mother would be more apologetic for how Lou ran my life, but she isn't. Romana thinks that somewhere along the line, my mother really came to believe that Lou was in the right, regardless of my feelings about it, because she just can't seem to see it the way that I do. We joke that perhaps she has Stockholm syndrome and simply is the way she is now after so many years with Lou that she can't change. And neither Romana nor I ever think that she will.

But, nonetheless, I would suggest to others that you keep an open mind to some extent when you don't know all of the facts for sure, and give as much benefit of the doubt as possible. At the time though, I needed to be angry with both of them to move past where I was. And Romana needed to believe that at some future time, my mother would support my feelings as a good mother should. These feelings kept us both from feeling too crazy and able to be optimistic about my future relations with my family.

Back to my own life. I want to let people know how good it felt to live on my own again, free from the breathing problems. I gave much thanks to God. Looking at my new home with all the things in it that I had picked out, I felt overjoyed. It felt like putting up with all that stuff in the group home, and the years of isolation at Greenstone, had been worth it.

Chapter 7

The Conservatorship
(How I came to find my attorney
and Bill on the path to freedom)

When I moved into my apartment, I had told Romana that after I had been living there for one year, I wanted to see about buying a home of my own, as I strongly felt that paying rent was the same as throwing my money out the window. I wanted a good investment for the home I paid to live in. That was one financial goal I had set for myself. After one year, we did indeed tell my family I wanted to buy a modest home, but Lou refused, saying I did not understand what it meant to own and take care of a home, and all that was financially involved with it. I was very upset, angry, and frustrated. It wasn't like I had no one to help me with this either. I had an excellent support system through Choices, ALTA, and MORE. This was *my* money, not his! I wanted a home of my own instead of throwing money out the window—as I considered renting to be. I became very disgruntled with Lou at this point, but I was still afraid of him or confronting him about what I really wanted. I was afraid to rock the boat very much myself. I was terrified of the possible repercussions if I made Lou mad, so I just let things be, even though I was extremely unhappy about it.

In the meantime, my speech therapist at MORE had suggested that I would benefit from a communication device. I felt this would assist my independence. With it, I could communicate when Romana was not around to interpret sign language for me. I would also be able to make phone calls and have something to communicate with in case of an emergency.

So, Romana took me to the University of California at Sacramento State to the Assisted Communication Device Center. We met with the head of the center, Tom Gray. I was put through a series of tests to see which device I would be best suited for. I found one that I liked a lot. The

Dynavox. So we told my family about it, and Dr. Gray communicated with Lou about it. The communication device would cost about $3,000. Lou refused. He said he could get a clock that talked in several different languages for about $25 and "why should this device cost so much?" His excuse was that he was sure the center was just taking advantage of disabled people by overcharging them. However, the device was really an advanced talking computer with a touch screen. I could touch it and it would talk for me by using pictures that I could pick out. So the clock and the computer were not remotely the same things, and Dr. Gray was very sorry that Lou had disallowed it.

So, I was upset that Lou had now refused to let me use *my* own money for two things that I felt were very important to me. I wanted a home of my own instead of a rental and a way to communicate independently. I was very frustrated that I was getting only $800 a month. Lou was in control of all of my money and spending the rest of it on I don't know what. But it wasn't me, at least not that helped my life on a daily basis, or that he ever told me about. But I was still afraid of upsetting Lou and having him move me away from my wonderful home and all of my friends and work and the support system that was helping my life run smoothly and independently.

Then, one day in the mail, I got a copy of the accounting of my estate. I am sure that I got this in error, (although in retrospect, I suspect I should have been getting one for years) but as I could not read or understand it, I showed it to Romana. She looked at it and did not quite understand it either, as it was quite lengthy and complicated, and she is not a numbers person, but a people person. So she suggested we take it to the accountant at Choices. The accountant looked it over and said she thought the numbers were off—significantly. The accountant suggested that I get an attorney to look into the handling of my estate. At the time, I also had a volunteer who helped me with things. Her name was Dorothy Stearman. I would stop by Dorothy's home on my way home from work sometimes, and she would help me with things, like hemming new pants for me, and I would move heavy things around for her. She was very loving and protective of me. When all this came up, Dorothy was sure I was being taken advantage of, and she wanted to help me. So she said she would look around and see what she could do to help find me a good, honest attorney who would help me sort out the truth of things. Dorothy had a friend who knew everyone in Placerville, including attorneys. She called her friend Christina on my behalf, who did indeed know a good and honest attorney. An appointment was set, and Romana and I went to meet with Bruce Kimzey. I think this was around March of 1993. This was two years after Romana and I began working together.

This would turn out to be one of the most important meetings of my life. Bruce looked at the paperwork and verified what I had suspected for years—that my money was being mishandled. I was terrified that if Lou found out that I had gone to an attorney, that he would take me away from my home and put me someplace where people did not understand me, or even worse, lock me up at their home again where I would have no way to communicate with my support system. I was also afraid that maybe I would be locked up in an institution, as he had threatened to do for years whenever he wanted me to cooperate with him. Romana realized that I was very upset about something, and kept asking until I told her this was my fear.

Bruce then said that he could file something called an "ex parte" order, which I didn't quite understand, but Bruce said this meant that Lou could **not** move me without the specific permission from the court, and that as my attorney, he would have to be notified where I was and that he would do his best to come rescue me. The only exception to my being moved away from my home would be if it was expressly determined by a doctor to be medically necessary to my continued physical well-being. This was an enormous relief to me! For the first time in years, I was not afraid. I was still concerned, but at least now I felt I had some sort of protection from Lou. Bruce asked me if I wanted to change my conservator, and I said a resounding "*Yes!*" I didn't have much money for an attorney, but Bruce said that was OK; he would take a small fee up front, and then work on commission, as he was confident that he would be able to help me.

Now, we had to find someone who would be my new conservator—someone I could trust who would help me with my money, teach me to understand the investments that I had, and would listen and interact with me about how I wanted to spend it. I didn't want someone who would just agree with me, but would show me what was the best way to handle my money. I certainly didn't want to make any mistakes with it if I could help it.

Bruce told us that he had a friend, Bill Cody, who had been the guardian of El Dorado County for some fifteen years. He said that Bill had retired recently from that position, but that he might be willing to take me on as a private conservator case. It would take a very extraordinary person with impeccable qualifications for the court to choose him over my stepfather, since family is usually the first choice. Bruce then arranged a meeting with Bill a few days later, and I liked him right away.

We met at my house so that I would feel comfortable and Bill could get a chance to meet me in my own surroundings. Bruce explained my situation to Bill, who became indignant at Lou's treatment of me. He looked over the accounting and again verified what I had been told, that my estate was being grossly mishandled. Since he had been the guardian of El Dorado County, he also knew all of the conservatorship laws, and he could see right off that Lou had already broken them by comingling my monies with the families, and this is expressly forbidden in conservatorship law. Bill said some of the investments were very bad ones and that he was a bit shocked that the court hadn't done something about it in the past. He then agreed to take me on as a private case. This was one of the most joyous days of my life. At long last, there was light at the end of my tunnel.

We want to make a comment here. For years, the court, with no questions asked, had approved the accountings that Lou had been filling. However, everyone on my team who looked at the accountings could see right off the bat that something was terribly wrong with them. How is it that they could all see it, but the court who was supposed to protect me and my estate rubber-stamped this fiasco for years and years without ever stopping the financial abuse that Lou subjected me and my estate too? We later found out that there had been one point where someone in Stanislaus County did almost cause Lou to be removed as my conservator, but somehow he managed to talk his way out of it, and then it was never looked at again. Because previous courts had approved the accountings, the court, when it did look into it, only went back for two years. By then, Lou had cleaned up his act knowing that his handling of my estate would be looked at for financial abuse. I hope that in the future there will be greater scrutiny of the estates of the disabled and seniors, and I hope that this book will help that to happen!

I also realize that there is a lot of political manipulating going on behind the scenes. And as an attorney friend told me, once one judge approved the accounting that wasn't quite right, then another and another, any other judge in the future is going to be reluctant to say that the decisions of the past judges (whom they are most likely friends with) were wrong. So again, it is easy for this to snowball and easier for them to just ignore and hope no one really realizes it. And most likely, they didn't realize that things were not quite right either. I also understand that the judges are very busy with high caseloads and often will take the word of whoever processed the accounting that everything in it is correct. The other person that the judges take to word of is the person from the probation department who is supposed to interview the conservatee. In my case, I don't remember any of those interviews that were supposed to take place until around 1992, when a probation investigator came to talk to me at MORE. I told him then that I wanted to change my conservator, but when I got my copy of the review from that department, after the judge had seen it, there was **no mention** of my request. So where did it go? How could he leave something that important out? I had been very clear at that time, and there were several of my support staff at that meeting with me, and we were all quite surprised to see that such a vital request appeared nowhere in the paperwork. It said I was satisfied with the job Lou was doing, which we all had known I was not. But when I found out, it had already been approved by the judge and too late to rebut at that time. So I suppose that the judge took it as written. Therefore it would seem easier to simply approve it as written rather than reading and evaluating the entire estate, especially one as large and complicated as Lou had made mine. But, that *is* what is supposed to prevent what happened to me.

Something else that would have helped a lot would have been if I had had my own attorney assigned to me as is being proposed by the recent conservatorship hearings. An attorney who represents the conservatee would be one of the best things that could happen. So much of what did happen to me would have been alleviated if I'd had one, someone to watchdog Lou and keep an eye on him and what he did with my money. I think my money would not have been plundered by Lou the way it was if I'd had my own representative. And I do hope that that becomes law soon!

Back to my story . . .

Meeting Bill was both good and kind of scary. In the past, my life had had many ups and downs. People I thought I could trust, I later found out that I couldn't. I liked Bill very much but also felt that I had no choice. I now had to trust Bill and hope that he wouldn't turn on me like my stepfather had. I felt on a deeper level that Bill and I had really connected heart-to-heart.

We met with Bill and Bruce several times to devise a legal game plan. One of the problems we were having is that the case was in Stanislaus County, which seemed to have some difficulty keeping its legal act together. There were many delays and oversights that caused further delays. For instance, a hearing date was set for us in October, but due to an "oversight" (in the words of the public defender), no notice was sent to us of the date of the hearing. The court continued the hearing until November 3, 1993.

A hearing was held on November 29, 1993, where the judge granted my petition to transfer the case to El Dorado County. Unfortunately, the judge thereafter changed his mind, apparently for the sole reason that my stepfather had appealed it being moved. My feeling is that he also had a relationship with some of the legal people in Stanislaus County and did not want it moved to El Dorado. I think that as I discussed before about the "rubber-stamping" of my estate by Stanislaus County judges, that perhaps Lou was afraid that the El Dorado County judges would not be so inclined to go along with the Stanislaus judges because they were in a different "clique." And attorneys also often have more sway with judges in their local community as opposed to being an attorney from another area. I also think that because Lou always said I was going to die at anytime, he used that to convince the judges that it would be easier for him if the case stayed in Stanislaus County. It seemed that Lou fought too hard not to move the case for it to be just about driving.

I want to go into the brilliance of Bruce's legal plans for a moment, because to this day, I still see them as quite wonderful. For instance, the reasons he used for my case being transferred to El Dorado County. The best reason was that I can't talk, and my stepfather had not come to visit me for a couple years and refused to let me buy the communication device that would have let me communicate with him. So how was I supposed to communicate with him? As my conservator, he was supposed to meet with me at least once a year. Bruce also brought up the fact that Lou was seventy-six at the time and that I was much younger and that it would be in my best interests to have the transitions accomplished in an orderly fashion and at a cautious pace. He also brought up that I lived, worked, and owned property in El Dorado County (the property I owned with my parents was the Greenstone Ranch).

At the end of February, Bruce wrote to Mr. Bowman—Lou's attorney—bringing to his attention the fact that the annuity provided to me by the city of Modesto had been left out of the accounting of the conservator estate. The annuity was also left out of the gross income from personal property. Bruce demanded at that time that my annuity payment be made to me after that. This did not happen. Bruce also made a demand for a full and complete accounting as to where all the prior annuity payments made to Lou since the payments had started on or about January 1, 1982 had gone. In other words, where did all my money go for all those years? Lou never did send us an accounting of where it had all gone. The court would later order something called a "forensic" accounting that was supposed to find out where all the money went. In fact, the forensic accounting was required for only the last two years of the conservatorship. This did not cover all the years when Lou had my money coming in and I got a very small percentage of it.

In April of 1994, my case was finally transferred to El Dorado County.

Sometime in early '94, my mother contacted MORE workshop to ask about my living situation. I did not want anyone to talk with her about my life. She had refused to visit me all the times we had called and asked her to. Now she was going behind my back and trying to find out information from other people about me. I was afraid Lou would somehow twist whatever she learned and use it against me. I had Romana call Bruce and tell him that I didn't want anybody talking to anyone but him about my life. And he could only say that I was fine.

During '94, the fight for my freedom from Lou wore on. The preliminary forensic accounting ordered by the court was done, and it showed "a number of significant problems" with the manner in which Lou had handled and accounted for my estate. In particular was the co-mingling of my money with Lou's. The law forbids a conservator from co-mingling his own funds with that of the conservatee to assure that such conflicts of interest do not tempt the conservator as most certainly happened in my case.

Bruce felt strongly that Lou's conduct had exposed Lou to significant personal liability. Not only for the estate funds used by him personally, and not reimbursed, but also for damages and attorney fees under both conventional theory as well as under the then recently enacted Elder Abuse and Dependent Adult Civil protection Act of 1992, which is contained in the California Welfare and Institutions Code at sections 15657 et seq.

Bruce said that I was entitled to **all** profits from my estate, no matter how skillfully Lou may have handled it. Lou, on the other hand, felt completely entitled to using my money for other things because he felt he had made a profit. The court said however that Lou was only entitled to the amount the law allows in the Probate Code, and not a penny more.

It was Bruce's intention as my attorney to trace back and collect where appropriate and lawful, all funds owing to my estate, which had been removed, depleted, or unlawfully "borrowed" by any persons, including my stepfather. It was also his intent to seek a judicial determination as to whether my monthly annuity payments, which were not originally included in the court's evaluation of the value of my estate, and then not ever properly bonded, should not ever have been controlled or utilized as part of the conservatorship managed by Lou. In other words, Lou did not include my annuity payments to the court when the court looked at the value of my estate. So, this was a difference of several thousand dollars a month for several years. This was about 13 years worth of money. In our estimation, it was roughly about $280,000.

On 1/11/1995, almost two years after I had my first meeting with Bruce, the court changed my conservatorship to a co-conservatorship, with both Lou and Bill Cody as co-conservators. This did not work out. Lou not only did not cooperate with Bill, he fought him on everything every step of the way, frustrating Bill over and over. I continued to be very frustrated about my situation, and we went back to court yet again to ask that Lou be completely removed as my conservator. After eight more months, Lou was finally dismissed as my conservator, and Bill Cody was appointed as the sole conservator of my estate, and I no longer had a conservator of my person.

To get to this point, however, there was first a dramatic scene in the El Dorado County courthouse. We were standing in the hallway outside of the courtroom waiting to go in when Mr. Bowman (Lou's attorney) came over and wanted to talk with Bruce privately. They went over into a corner to talk. I could see that whatever Mr. Bowman was saying to Bruce was upsetting him a great deal.

Bruce then came over to us (Bill, Romana, and myself) and said that through Mr. Bowman, Lou had said he would stop fighting me on the conservatorship change under one condition. Which was that I agree not to go after him for the monies that were shown to be missing from my estate (due to his negligence), which both Bruce and I considered embezzlement. And that I agree not to pursue criminal charges against him for mishandling of funds. Bruce felt sure that we ultimately would win if we continued to fight. I asked him how long that could take, and he looked sad when he said "Years and years, and Lou would be using your own money to fight you, and that could cost you thousands more." He then explained that at the end, Lou most likely wouldn't even have the money to pay me with because he did not have a bond to cover the monthly annuity since he never included it in the estate. Hence, Lou didn't have the insurance to cover the cost of reimbursing me for all of my money that he used for things other then me. So the best I could have hoped for would have been the justice of sending Lou to jail if the trials had been successful. And because Lou was so old, a jury might not have even given him jail time. It would have certainly cost me a lot of money for an unsure outcome. I think Lou was savvy enough to have pleaded ignorance of the law, and even though that is not supposed to be an excuse, it would have cost me thousands of dollars and more years of going to court to find out, and still, maybe lose, or Lou getting only a slap on the hand. So, it was in essence a lose-lose situation for me. I was furious at Lou for putting me in this position, but felt I had no choice but to let him have his way and agree not to go after him either financially or legally. This was very hard as hundreds of thousands of dollars of my money had been misused and now I had to just give up getting it back. But it was worth it to have my freedom from Lou.

So, as I said in my forward, I don't agree with my mother and sister Stephanie that Lou was this straight-up honest man. Because if he was, he would never have had to make such a deal with me. He would have had nothing to fear financially or legally if he had done nothing wrong.

However, I was now finally released from Lou and his machinations. This was a huge step for me! I thanked God that I was now "free"! I now had no conservator of the person, which meant for the first time since my accident, I wasn't living life in fear of being moved or locked up. There was no one to threaten me anymore. It also was a huge compliment from the court to me, in that the judge felt I was living and running my life in such a way that I did not need the court as a watchdog over me, and I was determined to make as many good decisions as I could. I knew my support team had worked hard with me to get me to this point, and I wanted to make them proud of me as well as myself. I could finally live my life as I wanted. Bill was in charge of my money, which was fine with me. I trusted him, and he worked hard to teach me about my investments and where all my money was and to include me in all decisions with regards to my money. This was so very different from how my financial life had been in the past, but I greatly enjoyed my meetings with Bill and learning about all my investments. Some of the ones Lou had made were totally worthless though, and we just had to sigh and suck it up as there was nothing to do about it. The more Bill looked at it, the madder he got and the more aghast he was at how awful a job Lou had done with my money.

One of the other things that Bill did manage to do was to force my parents to sell the house in Lodi, which they had also bought with my money. It had been (against conservator law) comingled with theirs yet again. They then ended up moving into a small apartment. Which did seem like a just karma to me. They were mad at me for forcing them to sell the lovely house they had bought with my money. But at least now, I was going to be able to buy the home I had always wanted. They now had to live in a small apartment without using my money to make their lives more comfortable for the first time since the settlement from my accident. All those years I had lived in tiny, cheap places, because that was all that I could afford on the minute amount of money that Lou sent me to live off of from my considerable income. Finally, the tables were turned the right way.

Lou's last stab at me however was to sell the house in Lodi for a loss, which again, was against the laws of conservatorship, which Bill had told them **not** to do, but that is exactly what they did. It seems all along the way that Lou had a blatant disregard for the conservatorship laws and my financial well-being. Bill was furious that after he had warned Lou's attorney that the Lodi house should not be sold for a loss, that Lou did exactly that. But, looking back, it was worth giving it up for the long run. Lou was now, finally, out of my life. And, I had a life to get on with.

Chapter 8

I Meet Danielle
(And we play a dangerous game)

In the summer of 1995, I met Danielle Alexander, again. I had met her some years prior when I had been at a local dance. I was being harassed by some young adults, who were teasing me because of my disabilities, when Danielle stepped up and told them to stop. She was wearing a short red dress and looked like a million bucks. She then proceeded to dance one dance with me. I didn't see her again until 1995 when Romana introduced us.

Danielle's parents were considering enrolling her in the independent living skills services from Choices, and the executive director, Lynda Marinics, had thought I would be a good mentor for her. It seemed that during the intervening years, Danielle had also suffered a traumatic brain injury in a serious car crash that she was lucky to survive. It left her with a very delicate sense of balance because her equilibrium was damaged. She also had severe damage to her short-term memory and had to use a day planner on an almost hourly basis to do her daily tasks. She also needed to be reminded to look at it to see what she was supposed to be doing next. Her parents wanted to know if Choices could help her become more independent. Because I was the only client at Choices with a traumatic brain injury, and was living successfully on my own, I was the obvious choice to mentor her. She was beautiful, kind, and charming, and we became enamored of each other quite quickly. Her parents were nice, but her father was very domineering. It turned out we had New York in common. I had been born there and lived there until I was eleven or so, and it had been Danielle's dream to go to New York after she graduated high school to get a career and away from her controlling father. She figured that New York was as far as she could get away without leaving the country. She had been Miss Teen El Dorado and wanted to be a professional model in New York. Unfortunately, her accident prevented that from happening.

We fell in love quickly, and not long after we met, we became engaged. I had my neighbor Francis call Romana to tell her. Romana was a bit shocked by the suddenness of it and asked Francis if Danielle's parents knew. Francis told her "not only did the parents know, they were taking the couple to purchase the engagement ring." We now believe that Steven Alexander (Danielle's father) had his own ulterior motives for supporting our marriage. Mr. Alexander had a lot to say about how Danielle lived her life. He signed letters using the title of being her guardian, although Danielle was now in her twenties, and in the state of California, people under the age of eighteen have guardians unless the court has appointed them to have a conservator as in my case. Over the age of eighteen, one has to go to court to become the individual's conservator. He never provided any legal proof that the court had appointed him as her conservator or guardian to ALTA or to us. Her mother was also her in-home support service person, which meant she got paid money to take care of Danielle. Danielle also got money from Social Security Disability Insurance, so between the IHSS and the SSDI, the parents got a substantial amount of money for Danielle's care. This would all come into play later.

We were engaged for almost a full year. The wedding would be Greek Orthodox like the Alexander's. We went to extensive premarital counseling during that time. The church seemed very supportive of the marriage.

During our engagement, Danielle told me how desperately she wanted to escape her father's control. I communicated to her that I understood and agreed. I had been under Lou's control too long not to know what she was going through, and I was glad that she loved me, and glad to be able to rescue her from her father. We decided that we would cooperate with everything he wanted us to do during the engagement. Our plan was that once we were married, we would be safe and we could separate ourselves from her parents and be like other normal married couples with our own home, and he would not be able to tell us what to do anymore. But . . .

Mr. Alexander did not really want us to live independently, and after we had gone house hunting and found a home we both loved and found suitable for us, with the assistance of Romana, and the approval of Bill, we decided to purchase it. We had purposely looked for a home in Cameron Park because that was in the area that Bill and Danielle's parents lived. Bill was only a few blocks away, and her parents were only a couple of miles away. I think we might have liked a place further away from her parents on one hand, but we didn't want to be too far from Bill on the other. Our home was closer to Bill's house than to her parents, which turned out to be a good thing in the end.

Bill, doing everything the way it is supposed to be done, petitioned the court for and received permission to buy the house.

Not long before the wedding, Danielle's father became quite irate about us buying the house and wrote a nasty letter to Bill, saying that because the house had propane, it was "tantamount to being a death trap." He signed the letter as Danielle's guardian. Living in the Sierra foothills makes having propane, especially for heating, a necessity. There are times when the electricity goes out, sometimes for days on end, and having propane heat is the difference between being cold and warm, sometimes even life and death. Danielle got chilled easily, and I wanted to make sure she would always be warm. For a short time, we looked then at apartments that were all electric while we considered getting the house switched to all electric. Bill thought that Mr. Alexander was being controlling and ridiculous about it. Bill had had propane for years himself and knew how safe it was. But just to appease Mr. Alexander, Bill had the propane company come check it out, and the fire marshall as well, who told Bill that propane is actually safer than electricity.

We thought this would be the end of our problems with Mr. Alexander and the house, but that was not so. On the day that escrow was supposed to close, he went behind our backs and called my lending company, and told them that the roof was bad and unsafe. Everything was frozen and stopped while the lending company sent out a roof inspector, who of course said the roof had been recently replaced and was just fine. The purchase went through.

It was at this time that after many years, I said good-bye to my friends (who I now considered family) at the workshop and my job at Super Plumbing and moved into what would be our new home and began to prepare it for Danielle. It felt odd at first to not get up and go to work every day, but I had many other things that I was doing that kept me busy. My new "job" would be looking after Danielle. It was agreed that we (Suzi from the workshop and my boss Vince from Super Plumbing and myself) would all keep in touch, and we have to this day.

Romana took Danielle and me on extensive furniture shopping trips, and our house was then well furnished. We did have a good time with the shopping and preparation for our new home.

She also went through my closet and emptied out some of my most beloved polyester things. She said I needed a fashion upgrade. I didn't think so, but I wanted to make her happy. She said I was a fashion misstatement. I enjoyed clothes shopping with her very much. I am particularly fond of one time when Danielle joined me in the dressing room, much to Romana's profound distress. She wasn't in there very long but it was nice. We took a few risks that way. We used every opportunity we could to get to know each other better. Romana was particularly aghast when I told her that Danielle had been giving me oral sex in her parents' house while they were in another room watching TV. She said we were taking dangerous chances. We felt we were entitled since we were engaged, but I agreed to try and be a bit more discriminating. We both really had incredible chemistry together and used to like to tease each other to build up the erotic energy. Needless to say, we were both very horny all the time.

Several months before we got married, Danielle was assigned a volunteer from Choices to help round out her social life some. Danielle's parents had isolated her so much that she had no real friends who came to see her. She had related the same experience that I had had of losing many of my pre-accident friends. They just didn't know how to be around us after our accidents. This is unfortunately far too common. And very sad. Romana was also the volunteer coordinator for Choices, and when a very nice lady in her middle forties signed up looking for someone to spend time with as a special friend, Romana's first thought was of Danielle. Especially since Danielle was going to be getting married, Romana thought a nice married lady for Danielle to be friends with and who could take her on outings away from her parents and talk with her about life, love, and intimacy would be a good thing. The two of them hit it off wonderfully. Valerie loved spending time with Danielle, taking her to lunch and the movies and talking about Danielle's fears as a virgin bride. Danielle used the time with Valerie to ask lots of questions about married life and being a good wife. Danielle was also always anxious to get out of her parents' house as much as she could, and she loved the outings with Valerie. They quickly became close friends, and it was clear that Valerie had many of the same concerns the rest of us did about Danielle's father's controlling of her. Valerie also witnessed Mr. Alexander's overly controlling behavior toward Danielle, and this only served to make her more anxious to help Danielle in any way she could. Mr. Alexander also sometimes tried to cancel Valerie's outings with Danielle, but Valerie never took no for an answer and would just show up anyway. Danielle was also clear with Valerie about her desire to get away from her father. She told her about wanting to move to New York to get as far away from him as possible, and that as much as she loved Todd, she was also marrying him to get away from her dad. Valerie understood this and supported Danielle in every way that she could, even braving Mr. Alexander's difficult behavior to do so. She became a very staunch supporter and advocate for Danielle. She was always concerned about Danielle's happiness and well-being.

The arrangements for our wedding progressed, although I was not happy with how it was going. I wanted to include my many friends and peers from MORE and other places, but her parents said they didn't want "those kinds" of people at the wedding. I offered to pay for the whole reception so that I could invite whom I wanted, but her parents still would not let me invite whom I wanted. Because I wanted to marry Danielle, I agreed to "kiss ass" and to just have my professional support people be there. I had wanted my boss, Vince, to be my best man, but they would not let me do that either. They said that only a member of the Greek Orthodox Church could be at the altar, and they would pick who it would be. I didn't even get to meet him until the wedding. On the outside, I seemed to accept this calmly, but on the inside I was furious and couldn't wait until her parents had no more say or control over our lives and decisions.

As for our honeymoon, Danielle's parents had "great concerns" about us taking a trip by ourselves. We had decided that we wanted to take an Alaskan cruise. The only way we could take the cruise was if Danielle's parents accompanied us. This was not my idea of a "honeymoon," but I was willing to make whatever arrangements I needed to make it happen. They didn't have the money for it, so I bought them their tickets as well. It made me sad and frustrated that we could not go alone, but I smiled and cooperated so that Danielle and I would get some sort of time together.

The wedding day came on 8/26/1996, and all went well. Romana, Bill, Bruce, Lynda Marinics, Suzi, Vince, Valerie, and other Choices and MORE staff attended on my behalf. I had Lynda and Bill there to represent my parents since I did not want mine there. Danielle had her sister and family there. Danielle's father made a very nice speech about how happy he was that we were married and how we were "meant to be together."

We took our honeymoon trip, and everyone had a good time.

But . . .

I had not told Romana and Bill that in the months before the wedding, Mr. Alexander had been pressuring me to make him my conservator instead of Bill. I knew I wasn't ever going to do that, but for the sake of marrying Danielle, I let him think that I might. I kept putting him off until after the wedding, when I figured that with all the legalities done, he wouldn't have power over us anymore. I was wrong.

After the wedding, we moved into our new home. Things went wrong from our first days there. There was something about Danielle that her parents had not warned me about, nor told anyone else about. It was a very dangerous behavior, and I was shocked to find myself dealing with it. It came to light when Romana was checking my prescription medications in my lock box. I opened it for her, and she was surprised to find about six pairs of scissors in it. They were all kinds of scissors. Big ones and little ones. When she asked why, I told her that I had discovered Danielle cutting her eyebrows with them. Not just the hair, but chunks of skin too! Sometimes she cut herself till she bled. So I had been forced to take all the scissors I could find in the house and then put them in the only safe place I knew where she could not get to them. I was concerned about her parents saying I wasn't taking good care of her. Now this was obviously not a new behavior. She must have been doing it in the years after her accident, but her parents never warned me to look out for this. It really scared me, and I told her not to do it, but she continued at every chance she got. This was the first sign that I had that she had some mental health issues that I was unaware of and that her parents had hid from me.

Our main problem, however, was her parents. The Alexanders insisted on coming over to our home at least once a day, if not more. Mr. Alexander acted like our house was his. He would come right in without knocking if the door was not locked. He would adjust our central air system without talking to us about it. He would scold Danielle if she was not wearing a sweater. He told us what foods we should eat. He started calling our Choices instructors and canceling our appointments without telling us. He flat out lied and said that Danielle was sick when she was not. When we wondered why our instructors did not show up and called Choices, they told us that he had called and said either Danielle was sick, or we had other plans, or some other excuse. He would drag us to the senior center for lunch instead. I hated going there. The people were nice enough, but it is not where we, as thirty-something young adults, wanted to be.

Valerie would still come and do outings with Danielle sometimes. The two of them would go to lunch and the movies, and they had a good time together. I was always glad to see Valerie, and I know how happy she made Danielle and how much Danielle looked forward to doing things with her.

Sometimes they would make cookies together or do arts and crafts projects together. I enjoyed hearing Danielle tell Valerie how happy she was with me and how much she loved me. I always knew that Danielle would have a good time and be in safe hands with Valerie. I also knew that Valerie was someone that Danielle could talk to about intimate things, and that also made me happy.

Besides Romana, there were two other instructors working with us now. They were a married couple, and they were good role models for us. They would take us shopping sometimes and cook with us as well. Danielle's father would also cancel appointments with them unbeknownst to us. Then there was an "incident" with them on October 31. We were supposed to have gone shopping the previous week, but Danielle had been truly ill, so it was delayed a week. We went shopping for a patch kit for our couch and the ingredients to cook curry chicken with Robert and Adrian. When we returned, Danielle's father was backing out of our driveway extremely fast. He stopped the car, got out, and started yelling at Danielle for not having a jacket on, and then yelled at the instructors saying that Danielle was sick and was not supposed to go out. It made me angry when he scolded us like we were toddler children, especially in front of other people like that. The instructors said that Danielle hadn't mentioned anything about being sick that day and that she had wanted to go out. Danielle and I went into the house, and Mr. Alexander then talked to the instructors. I could hear him telling them that we were just children and didn't know any better about anything.

This made me very, very angry. When Mr. Alexander came barging into our home, I got even madder. I was so mad that I began yelling and shaking. I was mad because Mr. Alexander was always intruding into our home, adjusting the thermostat in our house, and treating us rudely like bad children, ordering us around and telling us what to do in our own home. I had been living on my own as an adult for many years now and had been making good decisions about my life. I had fought hard to get rid of Lou and him treating me like a child. I had essentially kissed Mr. Alexander's ass for over a year while Danielle and I were engaged, all with the expectation of finally being treated with respect and dignity and like the adults we were, not the children that Mr. Alexander saw us and treated us as. It felt like all the gains that I had worked and fought for from Lou was now being smashed back down by Mr. Alexander. I had been squashing my rage at his treatment of Danielle and myself for well over a year now, and this was *my* home, and I had finally had enough!

I must admit, I let my anger get the best of me. It was so pent up that I hit the wall next to the thermostat, and the cover fell off. I then decided the best thing to do was to isolate myself from Mr. Alexander at the moment, so I went into the bedroom and shut the door. I could hear Mr. Alexander asking, "What's wrong with him?" After Mr. Alexander left, I went out to talk with Robert and Adrian. I asked him why Mr. Alexander had been there in the first place, and they looked at each other and said that he had said he had come to take us to the Senior Center for lunch, and then shopping for more Halloween candy. I thought that if Danielle was too sick to go shopping for dinner, then she should be too sick to go to lunch and shopping for candy. But that was Mr. Alexander's double standard. Robert talked with me a bit more and told me that it was important I tell Mr. Alexander my feelings, but that I not lose my temper, as Mr. Alexander could then say that I was incompetent and couldn't control my temper. I told Robert that I didn't think telling Mr. Alexander would do any good, but Robert said, "Maybe not, but at least you could get it out of your system then and maybe you'd feel a little better." He then told me I had done a good job by going into our bedroom and not letting my temper get more out of control.

Bill arrived shortly after this, and it was decided that a meeting should be called with everyone involved. I wanted to tell Mr. Alexander how I felt, but not alone. Danielle also said that she wanted to tell them that she wasn't a child and wanted them to leave her alone. She said her father had always had control issues and she thought it was because he was so short.

It was this incident that caused us to call our ALTA caseworkers to have them come talk to us about what was going on. On 11/4/96, they came together when Danielle and I were home alone. We told them that her parents made us feel like babies, and that they were trying to control our lives in ways we didn't agree with. We wanted our instructors to help us with shopping and other things because they never lectured us and helped us be more independent, whereas her parents seemed to want to control us and make us as dependent as possible.

Prior to this for several weeks Danielle also began to have severe concerns about her parents trying to get her to go back home with them. She had overheard them discussing their finances and that they were not doing as well since she had married me. Danielle had been getting Social Security for her disability that her parents used in their family budget. Also, because of Danielle's disability, her mother had been getting paid by the state to take care of her for almost 24 hours a day, under In Home

Support Services. When we got married, because of my income, Danielle did not get or need the Social Security insurance anymore. And because she was my wife, I looked after her, she did not need her mother to provide the same level of care giving anymore. We feel this caused a definite financial problem for Danielle's parents.

Danielle's father had continued pressuring me to let him become my conservator instead of Bill Cody. I finally told him flat out that I didn't want to change conservators, I was very happy with how Bill was doing things. He was the best in my book! Mr. Alexander smiled and acted like it was not a big deal. Danielle was adamant about her concerns about her parents' financial difficulties to the point where during meetings with Romana, Bill, and myself she told us she was afraid that her parents would try to take her away. She mentioned this to the other instructors Robert and Adrian, and also her volunteer Valerie Walker. She brought it up every chance she got to. She begged all of us not to let this happen, and that if her parents did succeed somehow, for us to not leave her there in that nightmare, but for us to rescue her. She was counting on me and her support system to get her back if this happened. We all promised that we would.

After the meeting with our ALTA caseworkers at our home, a meeting was held at ALTA in Placerville on the 12th of November, 1996, with all the instructors, the Choices's program director, our ALTA caseworkers, Danielle's parents and therapist, and Bill. This was a week after the caseworkers had been to our house. Danielle and I had told our ALTA caseworkers in the meeting at our home that we wanted more time to ourselves. That we wanted to do some shopping with our Choices instructors and that we didn't mind seeing Danielle's parents a couple times a week, but that mostly, we wanted to be able to live more independently. We did not want to be treated as puppets on a string, which is how we both felt. All these things were brought up at the meeting. Danielle's parents did not agree with this and tempers flared some. Finally, her parents agreed to give us some space, but we could tell it wasn't what they really wanted to do. At some point during the meeting, they seemed to give up, smiled, and acted like everything was OK. Romana remembers seeing Danielle's mother lean over and ask her husband what they were going to do now. He patted her on the leg and told her not to worry, that everything would be fine. Romana had no idea what he meant by this, but remembers that it felt very ominous and that a chill went through her. It was at this point that her parents stopped arguing with us and everyone parted on good terms . . . So we thought. Who could guess what they had really planned to do to us?

Chapter 9

The Destruction of a Dream
(Or how our game backfired and
the system failed us)

I have a letter from Danielle, written to me on 11/11/1996, telling me how much she loved me, and how happy she was to be my wife.

Valerie Walker, Danielle's volunteer from Choices, had been continuing to spend time with Danielle and I, mostly Danielle. Valerie and Danielle had become quite close in the months since they had met, and in November, Danielle had expressed to Valerie several times her concerns about her parents and how afraid she was that something was going to happen. That they were talking about how bad their finances were since she had married Todd and they didn't know how they were going to make it.

On Sunday, November 24, 1996, ten days after the meeting at ALTA, thirteen days after Danielle wrote the above love letter to me, Danielle's mother came to take Danielle out shopping, which was sort of strange because we all normally went to church on Sunday. But this Sunday, they went shopping instead. Three hours after they left, Mr. Alexander called and told me that Danielle was not coming home. Ever. Click. That was all. I called Bill, and he came right over. I was agitated and tried to explain to Bill what had happened. When Bill arrived, he called Mr. Alexander who said that Danielle is not coming back, that they needed to protect their daughter. He said that I had given her too much medication and allowed her to get cold, that she had missed a doctor's appointment. He also said that we didn't have any food in the house, which was a blatant lie, because Romana had taken us shopping to Costco (as she had been doing with me for years) and we had lots of good food. Mr. Alexander then threatened that Bill was going to go to jail for making a doctor's appointment for Danielle when he, Mr. Alexander, was her "guardian," and he said Bill had no right to make that appointment. Mr. Alexander was just making excuses and lying to try and justify what he was doing for the sake of control and money.

The next day, 11/25/1996, at 10:00 a.m., Mr. Alexander and his son came to my house with a letter he said was signed by Danielle that said that I was to give her belongings to her father. But it didn't look like her signature to me. I called Bill, who came over. Mr. Alexander was very hostile to Bill and told him again that he was going to jail for making a doctor's appointment for Danielle. Bill had made the appointment because I was concerned about her health. Mr. Alexander said again that he was Danielle's guardian and that Bill did not have the right to make doctor's appointments. In fact, since he wasn't her legal guardian, I as her husband should now have had more legal rights to make those sorts of decisions than her father did at this point. I will go into this later in the book as to my thoughts and feelings about how the disabled can be treated unequally by the system because of their disabilities, and how their legal marital rights are sometimes pushed aside or denied by family members who want to control them. And how the system can go along with this if the disabled people do not have any advocates on their side to help them stand up and know what their rights really are.

But, back to the story.

The Sheriff's Department was called, and two deputies came and asked Mr. Alexander to bring more proof from Danielle before demanding entrance to my home. I told them that if Danielle would come, I would give her whatever she wanted. Bill asked Mr. Alexander if I or Sally, her ALTA caseworker, could speak with Danielle. He screamed, "She is not available!" After Mr. Alexander left, Sally Gradall and Susan Pool (Danielle's and my ALTA caseworkers, respectively) arrived, talked to me and the sheriffs, and left.

On the twenty-sixth and twenty-seventh of November '96, Bill tried to arrange to have adult protective services, accompanied by Sally, to go see Danielle. It was arranged but did not happen. Sally couldn't go because Mr. Alexander had discontinued services with ALTA allegedly on Danielle's behalf. I don't remember if it was by phone or letter, but it was never in person from Danielle to her ALTA caseworker. If it was by phone, then it was certainly Mr. Alexander because Sally never got the chance at any time to talk with Danielle herself. The reason that we felt that this was all Mr. Alexander's doing is because ALTA was the very agency that Danielle and I had asked to help us deal with her father's control issues. We had asked ALTA to have the meeting, and for them to help us intervene with Danielle's parents of which they were more than willing to do, and in fact, ALTA was very supportive of our striving for independence, the very thing that her parents did *not* want. So it makes no sense that Danielle would voluntarily discontinue services with the very people she had just reached out to for help to protect her from her family. It makes much more sense that her father would do this to isolate her from the people who had stood up to him in supporting Danielle's independence from her family. We know that he would call and cancel appointments with our instructors without our knowledge or desire, and so, since Danielle had told us all over and over that she was afraid of this very thing happening, we did not believe that she had done this on her own accord, but that her father either forced her to write a letter doing this, or simply did it himself since it was never done in person or on the phone by Danielle. Which certainly deserves some looking into in the future for how this sort of situation is handled by ALTA and other like agencies.

ALTA is a voluntary service, and Sally could have met with Danielle if this was something that Danielle wanted, regardless of her family's desires.

But because "Danielle" had discontinued services with ALTA, then there was nothing that Sally could do. On the twenty-seventh of November, a sheriff went out and talked with Danielle, who told him that she was going to file for divorce. I was shocked. My wife, who had loved me so much two weeks ago (according to both her behavior and the note she wrote me), now wanted a divorce? I knew that this was not Danielle's doing, and that this was the very thing she had warned us about, and that she had been terrified of happening—being under her father's control again.

We wrote letters to the district attorney and went to the Sheriff's Department, but no matter what we did, no one could or would help. It seemed a clear case of undue influence that no one would listen, too. My mother had told Bill that she had talked to the Alexanders and during the conversation had told them "that the social workers would take Danielle away from them, just as they took Todd away from her."

This served to upset Danielle's parents even more and make them more resistant to our getting back together again. That was the final straw for me as far as my parents were concerned at the time. If I never saw them again, that would be too soon! My mother has denied ever telling this to Bill, but I believe Bill.

Romana and I then went to the Greek Orthodox Church where Danielle and I were married. Danielle and I had gone for extensive premarital counseling with the priest for nearly a year. For Danielle's sake, I had converted to her religion. You'd think that this would have given me some standing with the church, but Romana and I had a hard time getting him to even agree to see us. Finally he did. I thought if anyone would help us keep our marriage together, certainly he would. I asked him to provide marriage counseling for us, but he refused. He said that the Alexanders had been coming to his church for a long time, and that they were great supporters of it. He said that he realized that Mr. Alexander could be very dominating, and he didn't think I had done anything wrong. But he just wouldn't help. I was angry and sad. I had taken my marriage vows very seriously and never planned to divorce. I just couldn't believe that he wouldn't help. Needless to say, I never went back. It was apparent that money from the Alexanders was more important to him than my marriage.

Another thing we tried was a session with Danielle's therapist. I had agreed in advance to pay for it. It was supposed to be with Danielle, but after we got there, we were told that she would not participate. It was just Romana and I, and what was the point in that? Other than I got to tell her therapist how I felt about things, but this was not a therapy session for me. I had my own therapist to help me deal with my pain over this whole episode. This was supposed to be a chance for Danielle and me to talk about the reasons that she wanted a divorce. I had agreed that I would not fight the divorce anymore if she would have this meeting with me and told me face-to-face that this is what she really wanted. It would have been hard, but I would have let her go. I would not have gone if I had known in advance that she was not going to be there, as I would have seen it as what it was—just a painful waste of time. The therapist was nice enough, but it appeared to us that he too was under the parents' influence, and that he was not open-minded, nor that he was willing to help us reunite or save our marriage either. It just ended up costing me more money.

The only person outside of Danielle's family to see her alone after she went back to her parents was Valerie Walker. Valerie had also promised Danielle that if her parents did take her away, that she would do everything she could to get Danielle back. So when Danielle disappeared with her parents, she became extremely worried about her and wrote letters to Danielle and her family, called them repeatedly, and did everything she could to see Danielle. She felt that she had a special obligation to Danielle because Danielle had been so worried when Valerie was with her the day before her parents took her away. She had specifically told Valerie that she was afraid that her parents were up to something, and she was very angry with her mother. Danielle had asked Valerie to help her if her parents took her away, and Valerie had promised that she would. So Valerie tried everything to connect with Danielle. But Danielle's parents blocked her at every turn. They even had Danielle's divorce attorney threaten her with a restraining order.

Finally, in desperation, Valerie went to the senior center where she knew that Danielle's parents often took her for lunch. Valerie saw their car out front and knew they were there. She carefully watched until Danielle's parents were at another side of the room before she snuck over to sit down next to Danielle. Danielle appeared to be glad to see her, turned to her, and said, "Have you seen Todd, how is he?" Valerie replied, "He doesn't understand why you left, he is worried about you and is heartbroken." Danielle then said, "Will you take me to him?" To which Valerie replied, "Of course!" Danielle stood up with Valerie to go, then said, "Oh, I guess I should finish my lunch first," and sat back down. At that time, Danielle's mother came over and told Valerie to get away from Danielle. Then Danielle's father spotted Valerie and hurried over to her. He told her she had to leave and that she was causing a disturbance. He started calling her all kinds of names and pushed her at which point the other seniors started getting upset. One of the volunteers came over and told Valerie that she would have to leave, and walked her out. She told Valerie that she was very sorry to have to do so and was sympathetic to both Danielle and Valerie, but that Valerie still had to leave. And *that* was the only time that anyone ever saw Danielle or spoke to her without her parents present.

In all of this, I would say the greatest failure was with the one agency that was designed specifically to protect the disabled from this very thing, and that is Adult Protective Services. I feel there was a major conflict of interest with the APS investigators themselves. The bureaucracy caused nothing but frustration and difficulty. ALTA social workers were sympathetic but did not have the authority to be aggressive toward forcing a meeting with Danielle. The APS worker, Carol Halk, who had been the Alexanders's In-Home Support Services caseworker for several years, was extremely uncooperative. She stated that "choices was known by her to be 'too biased toward the clients'." (How is *that* possible, I ask you?) She refused to go out and make welfare check for over thirty days, until Bill called her again and attempted to persuade her to at least have a private discussion with Danielle. Ms. Halk told Bill she would not give us any sort of information without a court order.

Carol had worked with the family since Danielle's accident as her IHSS caseworker. (In-Home Support Services authorizes payment for hours of services provided to seniors or the disabled for living assistance, such as cooking, transportation to medical appointments, cleaning, and a variety of other things.) Because Danielle was significantly disabled, she was authorized quite a number of hours. Bill Cody thought the income to her mother was roughly $450 a month. So, when the IHSS case manager would come for a home checkup, obviously the family would be on its best behavior. In my opinion, I don't believe that Carol ever saw any of Mr. Alexander's obsessive and controlling behaviors regarding his daughter. He knew how to behave when he needed to. So when Bill called in the complaint of "undue influence," Carol Halk told him that she was on the "other side," i.e. that she considered Bill, ALTA, Choices, and Valerie to be wrong in this matter and that she was supporting Mr. and Mrs. Alexander.

This statement expressed by Mrs. Halk is the opposite of what any reasonable person's idea would be of what one would expect from a social worker or APS investigator. Should there not be a requirement of "open-mindedness" for an investigation into abuse or manipulation of a disabled person? How can it be called an "investigation" when none of the factual evidence is reviewed, or the witnesses involved interviewed? She never bothered to determine any facts that we offered, nor attended any meetings, although invited. She demonstrated an appalling lack of understanding. Her attitude was condescending, patronizing, and judgmental in this matter. Her understanding and evaluation of the situation was unsatisfactory. Because she was at that time working with Danielle and her family, she had already established a friendly relationship with them, and we felt that this was a conflict of interest in making open-minded judgments about the Alexanders in this matter. Carol did not talk to those witnesses who had had the most recent and extended contact with Danielle while she was away from her parents. She would not listen to the fact that Danielle had told us repeatedly that she was afraid that her parents would try to take her way, and how she had made everyone promise to get her back if this happened. This proved to us that Danielle **knew** this was going to happen and that she needed our help. Bill later wrote to Carol's supervisor and never received a letter back. It is interesting to note that on one occasion when Valerie Walker talked with Carol, Carol revealed that Mr. Alexander had been reported in the past for possibly physically abusing Danielle while she was in the hospital. This report was allegedly made by one of the hospital employees and was in regards to a bruise on Danielle's arm. From my perspective, there was a karmic result for Carol. A few years after this entire episode happened, Carol suffered a severe brain aneurysm and was left in a permanent semi-coma. Now she is experiencing being disabled firsthand. I hope she has an honest family.

No matter what we tried, nothing worked for me to see or talk with Danielle. No one in fact was allowed to see her. I was left with no choice but to participate in divorce proceedings against my will.

One of the worst moments came when the judge said that he thought we should have an annulment because "they never should have gotten married in the first place." I was aghast and furious! How dare he say such a thing! What gave him the right to decide who should and shouldn't marry? No matter how hard Bill, Romana, Valerie, and I fought against it, the annulment proceeded and was granted. It is interesting to note that a few years later, this same judge was thrown off the bench for being crooked. Karma again?

There was nothing to do but go home and grieve. I was heartbroken. I felt that everything I had ever loved had been taken away. This was 1997.

Chapter 10

My Friends and Support System
(How they helped me through
the emotional aftermath)

As you can imagine, this was an extremely difficult time for me and my support system in some ways. All of them had been very supportive of my marriage to Danielle and had done their best for both her and myself. Romana and Bill took the loss of Danielle almost as hard as I did. They had promised her that they would not let this happen to her, but in the end, they had no more choice than I but to go along with the court's ruling. We all felt like we had failed in some way, but there was nothing to do but go on.

If left to my own devices, I most likely would have stayed home, curled up in a ball of self-pity and misery. It was very difficult to allow others to reach out to me at that time. I really didn't want to see or talk to anyone. All I could do was think about what had happened and how lonely the house was without Danielle. But, I did know deep inside that just staying around the house dwelling on it wasn't the best thing for me either

In retrospect, I have to say here that everything *has* worked out exactly the way it should have. Except for Danielle, whom I wish did have the more independent life she wished for herself. I wouldn't have believed I would feel this way about it at the time if someone had tried to tell me this then. So whatever you do, ***don't*** tell the person in deep emotional pain that it's all going to "be all right." They won't believe you. Wait until some time has passed and they can hear the wisdom of your words.

It was around this time that Romana introduced me to Frank Welch, who would become a dear friend of mine and of much help and support during this difficult time in my life. Romana was worried about my mental and emotional well-being and felt that having a healthy father figure around would be beneficial to me. She didn't want me to just stay home and stew about how things had ended up. So she tried to find things and people that would keep me somewhat distracted. She then introduced me to Frank. Frank was a volunteer at Choices. We would go to lunch together, and he helped me with some projects around the house. It was hard to go on, but I did have a good support network of friends who cared deeply about me.

One of them was my friend, Carolyn Todd. She was also a volunteer for Choices. She had gotten a small Dolphin RV Camper. She knew how much I loved the outdoors and Yosemite specifically. I had done photography of it when in high school, and I had wanted to go back ever since. I was very angry and depressed during this time, and so Carolyn suggested that I could use a getaway to Yosemite to give myself some space to heal. We went for a week and had a wonderful time, strictly as friends. Being back in Yosemite made me feel happy, calm, and more at peace with things. It gave me some space away for a bit and a chance to reset my mind and adjust to how things were going to be now. She gave me the opportunity to be alone in the serenity of nature, and while it didn't change things, it did help me to accept it better. This was a very important trip to me, and I am very grateful to her for taking me on it.

It was during this time that my volunteer, Frank, helped me to find a piece of property in Placerville where I could walk to town and be independent. I wanted to build a house in Placerville to partially get away from the memories of Danielle in the home we had shared, and also to be closer to town, my work, and my friends. Frank went to the Catholic Church and became aware of a property that the church owned and was going to be selling. Frank asked if I was interested in it, and I talked with Bill and Romana and we went and looked at it. It was a nice corner lot, across the street from a friend of mine. It would make a good place for my house, and it was also a great investment.

I was still pretty depressed from what had happened with Danielle. Romana had some silly notion that I should get myself a cat to keep me company and give me something to love and take care of. I used to argue with her about it. She mentioned the little cat that hung around the Choices offices and how much happier I looked when I was petting it. She was persistent and I was stubborn. Finally one day, a couple of months after the annulment, she was again harassing me about it, and I suddenly started to laugh and agreed. She asked me why and I pointed to her shirt, which she had forgotten had three cats on the front of it. So we went off to the pound. I sat in a room with a cat who came and climbed all over me, hugging and purring. I fell in love with the cat. She was a big fat tabby Manx. She had had her claws removed, which was a relief because I had been worried about my drapes getting torn up from cat claws. I took her to a vet for a checkup, and the vet said she had feline AIDS and that I should take her back. I refused! I had the money to take care of her, and she needed me. So I found a fuzzy critter to love. I called her Pat, which were my initials reversed. Pat was the beginning of my healing process.

Chapter 11

Carla
(How my friend's impending death
caused me to rise above it all)

This brings me to Carla. She and I had known each other for years and years. She was a dear friend. I had told her that as long as she smoked, we could only be friends. Carla had fallen off a swing when she was little, and so she had suffered something of a traumatic brain injury herself. She loved going to the state fair, and I generally enjoyed going with her. After my annulment, she and some other friends had tried to cheer me up.

Carla was an interesting individual. She could be very childlike at one time and very adult at another. One of the things I admired about her most was her love of children. While she never had her own, she still found ways to have relationships with them.

One of them was through the Christian Children's Fund. Carla didn't have a lot of money and squeaked by on what she did have. But, she would go out of her way every month to get a money order to send to the CCF for the little boy in El Salvador that she had "adopted." With as little as she had, she was still determined to share what she had with someone less fortunate. She would have Romana help her write letters to him and sometimes send him special toys. She was very devoted to him.

Her other interaction with a child was with her niece, Amber, whom she truly adored. Carla would save money to buy her things as well. Not a birthday, Valentines Day, Easter, or other holiday went by without Carla getting something for her niece.

Amber's parents didn't always get along well, and sometimes her brother would cause huge fights with his wife. When there was much yelling and things being thrown, it was left to Carla to realize how unhealthy this was for the child, and Carla would often take Amber out of the chaos of the house to a quieter place until things settle down. So in this case, it was the "disabled" person who had more common sense about the well-being of the child than the "able-bodied."

A couple of weeks after our state fair trip in September of 1997, Carla and Romana came to tell me that Carla had a serious brain tumor, and it was within a couple of weeks that she had surgery to have it removed. I was shocked out of my depression, and now all I could think of was that I wanted to help her. There was nothing I could do to help her physically, but I knew I had the financial ability to help her mentally and emotionally. I made it my personal project to help Carla be happy. She had had to move home with her parents and could no longer be as staunchly independent as she has been for so many years. I knew how hard that was for her to have to now live with her parents again. She had fought very hard to be independent. We had known each other at the group home, and one of the things we shared was that we had both hated being at the group home. Neither of us liked people telling us what to do, and it would just make us more stubborn.

Now, she had to give all that up and move home, and this was very difficult for her. So every Monday we would spend the day together doing different things. Sometimes going shopping, sometimes to Sam's Town, and sometimes to the movies.

We also had a couple of parties at my house, and she loved helping me entertain. She wanted me to go to some of her doctor's appointments with her and Romana. I had thought she was going to get better. Carla told me that she had decided not to have chemotherapy or radiation because the doctors had told her that it would "cook her brain," and she felt she was already disabled enough, and the doctors had told her the therapy would make her even more so. But they also said it had taken years and years for that tumor to grow, so they hoped it would take as long for it to grow back. But it didn't. Several months went by and Carla started having some minor seizures. She wanted me to go with her and Romana when she went for another MRI scan. Romana and I stood behind the technician as the scan progressed. It was very quiet. We could clearly see the screen. Romana and I looked at each other and knew. We could see on the screen that the tumor had already grown back and was getting bigger again.

About a month later, we planned to have another party at my house. We went to some party supply stores and Carla picked out all kinds of fun decorations for the party. I let her indulge herself to her heart's content. The money was a small enough deal to me for the pleasure that she got out of it. Lavender and dark purple decorations were what she ended up picking out; our two favorite colors would be the theme colors for the party.

The Monday before the party (which was scheduled to be on Saturday), we went to see Eddie Murphy in "Dr. Dolittle." I remember buying Carla lots of candy for the movie. It was a great movie and we all laughed a lot. Then we went to Denny's for dinner. As we were coming out after eating, Carla asked us when we were going to have dinner. I turned around and looked at the Denny's sign. She turned and looked at it and her eyes filled with tears as she said, "We just ate dinner, didn't we?" I nodded and she said, "Todd, I'm afraid I'm losing my memory." I signed to her that Romana and I would be her memory. We said good night and Romana took her home. That was the last time I saw her. She died peacefully in her sleep the next night. I was grateful that she had passed so quietly and before the seizures got worse. I had had seizures and knew firsthand how awful they could be. I was also glad that she didn't deteriorate more because she could have gotten much worse, and she was so afraid already. Her memorial was scheduled for Saturday, the day we were supposed to be having our party. So I offered to bring all the party supplies that she had picked out up to her parents' house for her memorial. They were very grateful. It turned out that Carla's brother had driven from Colorado for her funeral and used most of the money for his wedding to come to it. After the memorial, I gave him all the pretty party supplies to take back with them. It turned out that their wedding colors were lavender and purple! So they didn't have to buy anything for their wedding. Carla's parents packed up all the leftovers from the memorial and took them all to Colorado for the wedding! Carla was supposed to have been a bridesmaid at the wedding, and her brother felt like she was there with all the lovely party supplies that she had picked out. I think I am relieved that Carla doesn't have to have any more seizures and that she is with God and her grandpa. This was around July of 1998.

A small but interesting note: the Christmas before Carla passed away, she had fallen in love with a floppy eared bunny we came across at Costco during one of my monthly shopping trips. I got it for her, and she loved it dearly. When Carla passed away, Carla's mom asked Romana if there was anything of Carla's she might want. Romana, remembering that day at Costco, asked for the bunny. That bunny has been with us while we have been working on this book, and we feel that Carla's spirit has been with us all the while we are working on it. In fact, you can see that bunny in the picture of me with the binders. She is sitting off to the side of me. I wanted to be sure that she was in the pic of me so that Carla will always be remembered.

Chapter 12

I Prepare to Move On
(Getting ready for Kelli)

In retrospect, Carla was a bridge for me. She helped me cross over from the pain of my destroyed marriage and gave me someone else to worry about beside myself. She did something that my other friends and supports hadn't been able to do, and that was really get me out of myself. Because of the severity of what she faced and its life altering consequences, I felt the need to really be of help to her. She had also kept me from being too lonely because I had to focus on her and I was always trying to think of new ways to cheer her up and make her life as happy as possible.

She had been hostess at the parties I had at my house. She had been my friend, but not my lover, and I missed having a lover in my life. So after her death, I decided that it was finally time to move on from my experience with Danielle and find a wife. I still maintained the goal that I had given to Romana the first day that I had met her, and that was to have a family of my own.

I was thirty-seven and had expected that by this time in my life, I would be married with children. I was angry because I had expected that with Danielle before her parents ruined it all. In retrospect, I am very glad that Danielle and I did not have children because her parents would have made it a real nightmare, and who knows if I would have ever seen my kids. But to move on, my concern with Carla took precedence in my life for a while. But now, it was time to think about myself and find the wife I wanted.

I talked with Romana about it and we discussed the different women I already knew, but I felt none of them were the right ones. I knew I didn't want someone who had been born disabled, as I know firsthand how hard that life could be. I wanted whatever children I might have to have the best possible chance at a good life. So none of the women I knew from the workshop were good candidates. Over the years, I had been careful to not get seriously involved with women with genetic disabilities so that there would be less of a chance of having disabled children. I was aware that it could happen to anyone, but I wanted to lessen the odds of it happening to me and my future children.

This brings me to an incident that I am not proud of, but bears mentioning here. In fact, it's downright embarrassing, but I think that others might be able to learn from my mistake, so I have decided to include it here. This has to do with how people with disabilities can be manipulated and not even be aware of it. Especially if that person has low self-esteem like I did. It happened not long after I began my conservatorship battle and shortly before I met Danielle.

It started when I was walking home to my apartment one day with two bags of groceries. A lady pulled up in her car and asked if I wanted a ride home. I had no idea who she was, but she said she had seen me many times walking to and from Raley's with my groceries. She had her two children in the car, which I didn't really take notice of. It didn't occur to me that it was inappropriate behavior for a woman with two small children in the car to pick up a perfect stranger. After we got home and talked, it turned out she was trying to get a divorce and needed a place to stay. Can you guess what I did next? Yup, I offered her a place to stay and she moved in with me that night. Part of my reasoning was that I was very horny and she seemed interested in me sexually. I had taken the bus to a brothel in Nevada recently and found out how expensive it was to pay for sex there. Intercourse was $150 and oral sex was $50, so I had opted for the lesser. I was disappointed that I didn't get intercourse, but I was a cheapskate and didn't want to pay that much for sex. After I invited Cheryl to live with me, we had sex a lot, so I figured I was getting a good deal. Her two children lived with us also. Cheryl never came right out and asked for money, but she would phrase things in such a way that I readily offered it to her. Such as her kids needed this or that or that she was trying to save up money for this or that and of course I would offer to help her. I didn't realize how much this added up to. Also, her son was slightly disabled and I felt sorry for him and wanted to help.

So, while most of it was about sex, not all of it was. I hid how much money I was giving to Cheryl from Romana, as I knew Romana would disapprove of this. And was I right! I didn't want Romana to know until I felt I had gotten my money's worth of sex out of Cheryl. When Romana found out, she was quite upset. I didn't really understand why. Hey, I was getting lots of good sex and it cost me less then if I was going to Nevada, or so I thought. Cheryl moved in on Saturday, and on Monday it all came out when my neighbor Francis called Romana to express her concern about "the woman who was living with me and the noise in my apartment" when I was gone at work. So Romana came to see me, and my normally neat house was a major mess. She couldn't help but notice the women's clothes everywhere and the children's toys strewn all about. She was quite shocked. She asked me about it, and I reluctantly told her about Cheryl. She asked how we had met, and when I explained her picking me up in the car with her children, Romana got real upset. She said I was a stranger to Cheryl and that I might have hurt her children. I told Romana I would never do such a thing. Romana said she knew that, but how did Cheryl know that? And that it made Romana concerned about Cheryl's lack of good judgment. I still didn't quite understand. And to be frank, it wasn't until Romana and I got to this part of the book and she asked how I would feel if someone had my daughter in the car and picked up a stranger that I finally understand why she was so upset and how dangerous this could have been.

Anyway, I had asked Romana to get something out of my desk drawer for me, and she found two cancelled checks for $1,500, each made out to Cheryl. In the notation on one was "for divorce" and on the other "for a car." There was also a K-Mart receipt for $150 with panties and children's toys on it. She brought the checks and receipt to me and asked me about them.

Well, I told her how much sex cost in Nevada, and that Cheryl and I were having lots of sex so I figured I was getting a good deal. Romana was nothing short of aghast at me. She said I deserved better than that. I deserved someone who would love me for me and not for my money. I told her that I was lucky to be getting sex at all and she again disagreed. Romana said I was worthy of being loved as I was and that I shouldn't have to pay for it at all. She asked if I wanted to have a relationship or if I wanted a whore. I agreed I wanted a relationship. She also reminded me that I was in the middle of my conservatorship hearings and that it would make perfect ammunition for my parents if they found out that I was being taken advantage of in this way. I got mad at her at first and didn't really believe her. It wasn't until my attorney called me and seconded Romana's concerns about what was going on. He said I was endangering my court case with this behavior and how my parents could use it against me. I hadn't thought of that. I must admit I was thinking with a fairly narrow mindset at the time. Romana had had to tell her supervisor about the situation, and Nancy came out when Cheryl was at my house and confronted us both. I did not like the way Nancy handled it. She was extremely rude and obnoxious to Cheryl. She threatened to call Adult Protective Services and Child Protective Services on Cheryl, which was not too awful, but then she followed Cheryl out to her car, screaming horrible derogatory names at Cheryl in the parking lot of my apartment and in front of all my neighbors. I was very embarrassed and angry and signed for Nancy to leave. Romana was also shocked at her supervisor's behavior. Realizing I had made a judgment mistake was one thing, but it should have been handled quietly and privately. There was not cause for Nancy to go so off the beam and embarrass me in public that way. I told Romana that I wanted to file a complaint about how Nancy had acted and humiliated me in front of my neighbors. Romana agreed and said she needed to file one also for the excessive display of inappropriate behavior by her supervisor. I told the executive director of Choices that I never ever wanted Nancy in my house again. I was promised that she wouldn't be, and she never was.

This was just before Bill came into the picture. In retrospect, I'm pretty glad about it. I can't imagine what that sort of conversation would have been like. After Romana, my attorney, and I discussed the money I had been giving to Cheryl, I promised them that I wouldn't give Cheryl any more money and see if she stuck around just for me. When I told Cheryl that I wasn't going to be giving her any more money, she left the next day. So it turned out that Romana and Bruce were right and I was just being used for my money. I was a bit lonely again, but I had learned a lesson. That sex was not something that I should pay for. And while I wasn't really sure I would find someone, I was willing to see what would happen.

Another repercussion of my experience with Cheryl was the physical danger that I opened myself up to. This was something else that had Romana more than a little concerned. Cheryl had told me that both she and her husband had slept with a variety of people, males and females each, and while I know this was a stupid thing to do, I had unprotected sex with her. I know, I know . . . Looking back at it, I can only say again: I wasn't thinking clearly at the time. As a result, I had to go to the health department for an AIDS test and other venereal disease tests, one which was when they stuck a long Q-tip sort of thing inside my penis. It was both painful and embarrassing. I would tell people to not have unprotected sex unless you are married. I know now how lucky I was to not have caught anything. It's a good thing to listen to those that care about you. I am lucky that being hardheaded didn't get me killed or forever damaged.

Shortly after that, Danielle came into my life. While she was not in it for money, I believe her father was. And in looking back, I can see how keeping the secret that Danielle's father was pressuring me to let him be my conservator after the wedding from Romana and Bill was not a good idea either. Every time I have kept secret that someone wanted either money or control of my money, it has turned out badly. In retrospect, I wish I had told Bill and Romana about Mr. Alexander wanting to be my conservator before the wedding so that the behavior could have been confronted and either the wedding or what happened afterwards could have been avoided. It has been a hard lesson for me to learn that it's never a good thing when someone wants me to keep a secret that I shouldn't from those that really care about me. Thank God I don't have to worry about that any more!

The reason I have brought all this up with Cheryl is to explain why Romana was so protective of me and wanted to meet someone I might meet from the Internet before I did. By then, I had agreed that she was right. And Bill agreed too.

So because of all I had gone through and how much I had learned over the years, I finally felt ready to get married again.

Romana was very protective of me, and I had agreed to her condition that anyone I found on the Net who had sounded interesting and who seemed interested in me she would get to meet her alone first. This was because I knew others had tried to take advantage of me, especially Danielle's father. Romana did not want that to happen to me again.

Romana suggested that I might be able to find someone on the Internet that I could get to know. There were lots of other lonely people out there. I had my concerns because of my inability to speak and other disabilities. But Romana said she would help me. Sometimes I argued with her about my being able to find someone who would love me the way I am. I would tell her that no one would want me because I can't speak. She would tell me I was wrong and that while I couldn't speak, I could communicate and that the right person was out there waiting for me. I didn't believe her, but she was as stubborn as I was. We banged heads over it quite a bit. But after all, she had been right about the cat! She finally talked me into looking on the Internet just to see if there was someone I might be interested in. We read many ads, and there was one that I picked that I liked the sound of. So we answered her ad, and she wrote back to us. She didn't mind that I couldn't talk. So that was a good start. Romana told me I was not allowed to mention my money situation at all, as we wanted this person to want me and not my money. We would only say that my bills were taken care of.

OK, back to the person on the Internet. We wrote back and forth a few times, and she and Romana spoke on the phone as well. A meeting place and time was picked. She lived in Sacramento, and Romana agreed to drive down there to meet her. I was anxious and curious. Romana went to meet with her and liked her very much. Romana told her that I had many people who cared about me and that we wanted to make sure I wouldn't be hurt again. Kelli talked to Romana about her work at the Sheriff's Department working the graveyard shift. Kelli told Romana about her family that lived nearby and the house that she owned. This made Romana feel good about Kelli being self-supportive and not needing my money to survive. Also that she had a responsible job, was settled in the community, and was a homeowner like me.

As far as the meeting between them went, Romana has relayed to me what was the "moment of truth" for her, when she knew that Kelli was the right person for me. She and Romana had been discussing Kelli's work at the Sheriff's Department. Romana asked her how she felt about those folks getting arrested and working the graveyard shift. Kelli smiled and said, "I know I'm just not seeing them at their best." This was such an insightful statement into the kindness in Kelli's heart, that it was a clincher for Romana.

She came back and told me how wonderful she thought Kelli was. I was quite anxious to meet her for myself. But Romana wanted to meet with her one more time first. Then a meeting with me was set up.

When I first saw Kelli, I felt that this would be the right lady for me. She didn't mind that I couldn't speak, and I was greatly relieved. Then Kelli came to visit me at my house without Romana there. I felt like I had a lot in common with her for what I was looking for in a mate. I was lonely, and I didn't want to be alone anymore. Kelli felt the same way. It was the second time we got together that I asked her to marry me. And she accepted. We had been intimate with each other, and I felt we were well suited in that area as well. It was 99999999.9 percent great! We called Bill and talked to him, and Bill asked us to wait at least six months before we got married to make sure we got to know each other well. Kelli and I met with Bill and Romana several times during those six months, as we began to plan for the wedding and our future. We decided that I would move to Sacramento since Kelli was still working, and it would have been a long commute for her with the hours that she had at work. She also liked being near her family, and since I didn't have any to speak of, that was fine with me. I was a bit reluctant to leave all my friends and the support system I had there, but I felt Kelli was worth it, and Romana and Bill had both promised to come see me often in my new home.

We decided to have the wedding at Kelli's house. I had lots of patio chairs from my home in Cameron Park, and so we only needed a few more to have enough to sit everyone. Bill was my best man; Kelli's sister-in-law was her maid of honor. I did not tell my parents about any of this, as I did not want them to interfere in any way with my wedding or marriage as they had in the past. So, on the third of July 1999, I got married again. It has been four and a half years as I write this. It has been the happiest time in my life. I did at some point give Kelli permission to talk with my mother and let her know that we had gotten married. We even went and visited a couple of times. We also saw some of my siblings. But my family did not go out of their way to contact me very much.

Kelli's family, on the other hand, has adopted me as one of their own in every way. Both her parents, the brother, and sister-in-law that live nearby are in our lives on a regular basis. I love the life I have with Kelli. When we first got married, she was still working at the Sheriff's Department. I wanted her to quit, but she felt she needed to stay on until we got some of the past bills paid down. We wanted children and I felt she needed to be home for that, but I abided by her wishes to work for a while. We rented out the house in Cameron Park, so we didn't have to pay the mortgage on it ourselves. We discussed building on my property in Placerville, but we decided to stay near Kelli's family in Sacramento instead. We wanted to be near family when we did have children. After about two and a half years of marriage, I was finally able to convince Kelli to quit her job. I felt that the late hours she worked was a strain on her and would keep her from getting pregnant.

I was right.

Chapter 13

The End of My Conservatorship
(Thanks be to God and Bill)

Bill and Romana had continued to be closely involved in my life and watched how my marriage with Kelli progressed. We all had regular meetings together, Bill, Romana, Kelli, and I. I would also meet alone with Bill and Romana so that they were sure I was really speaking my heart and not being swayed by my wife. After the fiasco with Danielle and her family, they wanted to be really sure I was not keeping any secrets from them.

Once Bill and Romana were absolutely sure that she was not in it for the money or would abuse me in any way, they decided the time had come for us to discuss having my conservatorship dissolved. I felt that things had progressed well, and that Kelli was looking after me and helping me with my finances in good ways. So we discussed what it would take to have the conservatorship closed out. A final accounting was done, Bill showed us both everything we needed to know about my investments, and helped simplify them. He brought all of his files regarding me down, and we set up a filing cabinet for them. My investments were rearranged so there was less to do with them.

On March 3, 2000, my conservatorship of both the person and the estate was officially closed. The judge did ask both Romana and Bill to keep an eye on me and let the court know if anything changed that the court should be aware of. It is now December of 2003 as I write this, and things are only better.

The ranch that my parents had bought with me was refinanced by the purchasers, and we were finally paid off from it. We used that money, plus the money we got from selling the Placerville property, to pay off both the Cameron Park house and the house in Sacramento so we would no longer have any kind of mortgage. The rent money from Cameron Park goes into a special account in case we need to do something with it in the future. We also got some wonderful news in 2002 that caused us to decide to make some remodeling changes in our home in Sacramento.

With the bills under control and the houses paid off, I was finally able to convince Kelli to quit working and focus on us having a child. More than anything else now, I wanted to be a father.

Bill Cody's Thoughts on Conservatorships

This is to provide some information regarding the direct and passive exploitation of some conservatee's rights, both in establishing placement and particular dispensation of estates.

I served as the El Dorado County Public Guardian for nearly twenty years. Accordingly, I represented more than a thousand of both probate and LSP conservatee's. After a while, an unfortunate belief by the families of someone who had become incapacitated by age, mental disease, accident, physical infirmities, or myriad of other problems created a situation wherein the person could not provide for his/her essential elements of life without assistance or were unable to manage their own financial resources or could not clothe, feed, or house themselves. Neither could they apply for benefits or entitlements that would give them both financial and daily living assistance.

Consequently, the incapacitated, in the illusionary concept of family members, seems to be regulated to a perfunctory status wherein the conclusion seems to be that "they," the family, may as well use the assets themselves because the helpless person cannot utilize them anymore.

The person appointed conservator by the court had a "fiduciary" duty that requires that the surrogate decisions are made in the best interests of the person pertaining to the most effective and agreeable environment for comfort and care within the scope of the resources. The conservator must be prudent with sound judgment with the financial assets and subordinate his personal interests to that obligation in the event of a conflict. Unfortunately, the oversight and enforcement of the conservatorship functions, from my experience, is not well scrutinized. Much of the problem is created by assigning the task to some individuals who are not well qualified or sufficiently trained or is not able to empathize or understand the conservatee; consequently, the evaluation becomes a nuisance task, a "square filling" obligation that is not specific or comprehensive.

The problems do not only exist with social workers, which are assigned for convenience and are assumed to be capable, but also with attorneys who evidently do not refer to the codes or statutes that apply. This has been particularly apparent regarding the sale of conservatorship personal and real property. Particularly egregious are situations regarding the sale of real estate. It does not require a stretch of imagination to see that an unscrupulous person could manipulate the price and favor a friend or "straw man" and share the profit. The code requires an impartial and fair appraisal that, in my time, was provided by the inheritance tax referee and required a notice posted in the courthouse at least ten days prior to the sale with court-supervised "overbids" to the public.

I could provide specific examples of gross infractions that violated this provision of the code, but there is a confidential mandate that I cannot disobey. Consequently, I can recall many such negligent transactions that resulted in an unjust loss to the conservatee's estates, which in many instances were settled via compromise to expedite funds needed by the conservatee.

Although I have been retired for many years, it is quite apparent that the problems have not been corrected. In fact, it appears that the conservatorship process has now become a "bookkeeping" function that is anathema to my opinions that the surrogate decisions most importantly should be determined by knowing as mush as possible about the matters paramount to the conservatee.

September 27, 2009

Chapter 14

We Find Out Kelli is Pregnant
(1/2 way through the term)

In July, Kelli went to get routine tests done. They asked her if there was any chance she was pregnant, and she was sure she was not. But they decided to give her a pregnancy test anyway. You can imagine our surprise and shock when the test results came back not only positive, but that she was about eight weeks so. We went for a prenatal ultrasound checkup, and were even more shocked to find out that she was not eight weeks pregnant, she was eighteen weeks pregnant. Halfway through her term! We were both beside ourselves with joy! We immediately started remodeling plans for the house to adapt it to the new addition. We decided to have all the carpeting removed (except the master bedroom) and hardwood floors put in since that would be much easier to keep clean and less chance of allergies. We had the cat's room remodeled into a nursery, and we had a wonderful time stocking it with all kinds of delightful things for the baby.

Kelli's sister-in-law, who lives about half a block up the street from us, had had twins the year before, so we had gotten some exposure to pregnancy, childbirth, and babies. It was like a chance to have training wheels before our own child was born. Time seemed to race by as we prepared for the baby's arrival. Life looked different to me now that I was going to really be a father. I prayed for the well-being of our child. We had gotten one test result back that suggested there might be problems with the baby, but Kelli and I decided to ignore that and go on as if everything would be all right. We knew we would love the child no matter what its condition was. After we had been told about the baby's heart, we had found out from my mother that my twin sister and I had both been born with small holes in our heart that had healed up fairly quickly, and while it is genetic, I hoped that if our child was born that way, it would, in the end, be all right like my sister and I had been. All of our friends and family were thrilled for us, and we knew our baby would be welcomed into the world with not just our love, but theirs too. Bill and Romana were as thrilled as we were for us. So was Susie and Vince . . . all of my friends knew how badly I had wanted a child. In fact, the first day that I met Romana, I had told her that one of my goals was to have a family.

Now it was about to happen . . .

Chapter 15

December 16, 2002 The Birth of My Daughter Naomi Andrea Presley (The fulfillment of a lifelong goal)

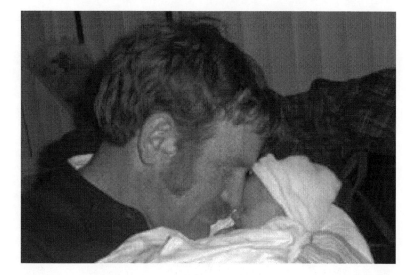

On a regularly scheduled clinic visit (Thursday), Kelli's blood pressure was up and down, and the doctor wanted to admit her to the hospital then. They let us go home with the promise to return the next day. The doctor then decided to induce labor.

We were taken to a "birthing suite" at UC Davis Medical Center. It was much nicer than I had thought it was going to be, and the staff there was the best! It took three days of labor . . . and I was getting scared for Kelli and the baby . . . it was taking such a long time. Kelli's blood pressure kept going up and down the whole time; it was in some ways a dangerous situation. But I held her hand and let her squeeze it as tightly as she needed to. Kelli was a trooper through it all. But finally, after all that, on December 16 at a little after 1 a.m., I was able to not just watch my daughter being born, I was even able to cut the umbilical cord. The baby cried, and I knew she would be OK then. I asked how her heart sounded, and they said it appeared she did indeed have a small hole in her heart, but they were sure she would be OK. And indeed, she was.

The first time I held her, I felt thanks to God for everything. They let me sleep in the room with Kelli and the baby, and then Kelli's family came to see us, and Romana came that night. I can say that it was one of the happiest days of my life. I was very relieved that she appeared to be healthy. Later checkups by the doctor would verify this.

As I write this, Naomi is less than two weeks away from being a year old. It has been a remarkable year. I have watched her go from being a baby to a toddler. She went from crawling to almost walking. She can pull herself up on things, and she is hard to keep up with because she is so active. She can be down the hall in a flash. She spent the first months in our bedroom and is now adjusted to her own room. I know she'll be not just walking soon, but running. She is a happy child who loves to sing. I used to be afraid that my child would not understand me, but I don't feel that way anymore. Right now, we are the same. I can't talk and she can't either.

UPDATE:
October 2009

Time has passed as we have worked on researching this book and working it all out into the story it has become.

Naomi will be seven years old in two months. She started first grade this year, and she chatters away like crazy. She is a good girl, well-spoken and highly intelligent. She seems to be way ahead of many children her age. Todd is also happy that she is left-handed as he is.(and Romana too for that matter)

We love her very dearly and she is a true joy in our lives. I still can't speak, but she understands me very well anyways. So, again, Romana was right when she said any child I had would understand me. Having two parents at home who love and look out for her has been a great benefit to her, and I thank God everyday for blessing me with this wonderful child and letting me be a part of her life.

Living down the street from her twin cousins has also been wonderful for her, and as I write this, she is off to spend the day and have an overnight with them. She had told Romana and I how the two girls fight with each other and that she gets in the middle and tells them to stop. My dear little girl has become the peacemaker, and I am very proud of her for that as well!

Having family so close by to be involved with has been superb. We have all managed to look out for each other and be of help to each other, and after all, that *is* how family is supposed to be. While sometimes I am sorry that my own family is not that way, Kelli's more than makes up for it. Even when things are difficult, we all pull together as a family, and again, I feel totally blessed to have Kelli and her wonderful family in my life.

With my personal life running so smoothly and happily, I want to devote the next few chapters of the book to dealing with my experiences with the "system" that I had to live with. The good, the bad, and the ugly of it. Along with my own observations and suggestions as to things that need to be changed and ways to make this difficult experience both better and fairer for others. And to make families more aware of how their behavior can affect the feelings of those that need to be not just looked after, but encouraged and supported to be the best that they can be in all ways. My family started out wanting the best for me, I think, but in the end made it a terrible and painful struggle. I hope that this book will open the eyes and hearts of many and let them feel my words and my experiences so that they can make more loving, if not harder decisions to support independence.

Chapter 16

In Legal Retrospect
(My thoughts on legalities and
humanity regarding conservatorships,
guardianships and payees and privacy)

From my experience, there are three kinds of "controls" that I have run across for myself and many of my peers. Those are conservatorship, guardianships, and payees. The first two have to do with one's rights and monies. The third, payees (for Social Security) *only* have a right to monies, but *not* rights. And many of the clients that I have known over the years thought that because someone was their SS payee, that also gave them the right to control their life and where and how they lived, which it does not. We will address the issues of these different sorts of legal terms and my experience with them.

First, here is the information on guardianships versus conservatorship from the state of California.

Difference between a Conservatorship and a Guardianship

Guardianship: **Many people confuse Guardianships and Conservatorships. A guardianship establishes an adult who is responsible for a *minor* child. *A guardianship cannot be established for an adult who cannot take care of themselves.* A Guardianship is a court process whereby the judge gives someone that is not the child's parent custody of the child or the right to control the child's property, or both. To become a guardian, you must file a petition, and the court has to approve it. In most situations, California law requires that minors have an adult who is responsible for them. If the court orders guardianship, it can be:**

- ☐ **Guardianship of the child's person (custody);**
- ☐ **Guardianship of the child's property (called "estate"); or**
- ☐ **Both.**

A Guardian of the minor's *person* has legal custody of the minor and is responsible for taking care of the minor's well-being. A guardianship of the minor's *estate* is necessary if the minor has substantial assets, such as an inheritance. Depending on your situation, you may need a guardianship of the minor's person, estate, or both.

Next, I want to point out that there are several kinds of conservatorships.

A. *Probate Conservatorships*

1) **General conservatorships** These are set up for adults who can't handle their own finances or care for themselves. These conservatees are often older people with limitations caused by aging, but they also may be younger people who have been seriously impaired—as the result of an auto accident, for example. These are also generally divided into two sorts of conservatorships: those of the Person, and those of the Estate.

2) **Limited conservatorships** These may be set up for adults with **developmental disabilities** who cannot fully care for themselves or their property, but who do not need the higher level of care or help given under a general conservatorship. Developmental disabilities include mental retardation, epilepsy, cerebral palsy, and autism that began before age eighteen. They also include conditions that are similar to mental retardation or that require similar treatment. For someone with more extensive developmental disabilities, the court may decide to set up a general conservatorship.

3) **Temporary conservatorships** These may be set up when a person needs immediate help. A judge may appoint a temporary conservator of the person or of the estate, or both, for a specific period until a permanent conservator can be appointed. A temporary conservator arranges for temporary care, protection, and support of the conservatee and protects the conservatee's property from loss or damage.

B. *Lanterman-Petris-Short (LPS) Conservatorships*

Lanterman-Petris-Short conservatorships are so-called because they are based on the Lanterman-Petris-Short Act, a 1969 law named after its sponsors in the California legislature. They are also called **LPS conservatorships**.

An LPS conservatorship must be created to arrange for certain kinds of very restrictive living arrangements and extended mental health treatment *for people unable to provide for their own needs for food, clothing, or shelter as a result of a mental disorder or chronic alcoholism, and who cannot or will not agree to the arrangement or treatment voluntarily.* Although a private citizen may be appointed an LPS conservator, the appointment process must be started by a local government agency, usually a county's public guardian or public conservator.

I don't know much about the LPS conservatorships, as that was not the kind I had. Mine were general conservatorships, so those are the kinds I am going to share my experiences about.

The general conservatorships are for folks that are disabled or considered incompetent by the court. Of the conservatorships, the first one is for the "estate" (which means handling the person's money) and another, of the person (which means control of their life and rights). A conservatee can have either, or both. I would suggest that the one that looks out for their welfare while giving the individual the most choices is the best. If someone can't handle their money well but can make a decent choice of where they live, then it would be best if they only had a conservator of the estate and **not** the person. Sometimes an individual will need both, but not always. Speaking as a person who has had both, I know that I needed lots of help in the years right after my accident because I was very fuzzy brained, but as the years passed, I got better, and after I got better and could think clearer, I really only needed a conservator of the estate and not the person. It would have been more accurate for me to have the conservatorship changed from a "general" to a "limited" because I was thinking better and could manage my own apartment and bills. As far as my estate went, however, and because of the amount of money I had and the complexity of it all, I did need a conservator of my estate to protect my money and me. As the years continued to pass, I could make better decisions about my life and where I lived and did not need a conservator of the person at all. Again, I think going with the least confining is best, better to start with one, then add the other later, if needed.

As a conservatee who has been inside the system and had a chance to go back and look at how my conservatorship was handled, I would like to recommend there be changes made to reflect what I have learned to better protect the disabled. One of those is, of course, that conservatee and conservator monies *not* be mixed in any way. This should be more strictly enforced, and there should be severe repercussions and cause for dismissal of the conservator if this rule is broken. In my case, Lou did this twice and nothing ever happened. I believe that this caused him to become more arrogant about how he handled my money as the years passed and gave him more disregard for the law and me. This caused us many problems later down the road. He felt like he was invincible and accountable to no one. He was reprimanded once by the Stanislaus County district attorney for comingling funds (and some other things that did not add up in the accounting), but it didn't make any difference to him, and there was no follow up by the DA to make sure he was doing things the right way. He sold (as ordered by the court) the ranch to separate our comingled funds, and in the next breath, turned around, bought a new place in Lodi, and comingled our funds yet again. Hence my point of view that he had no regard for the law. And he did it with malice aforethought because he had just been told by the court to *not* ever comingle our funds again.

Another suggestion I would make is that if a conservatee owns property that is for sale, then the loan should not be floated to the buyers by the conservatee's estate. In other words, a loan should only be done by a proper financial institution such as a bank or mortgage company, and not loans from a private party.

My parents floated the loan on the ranch to a private party, and then the people stopped making the payments after many years. They left the ranch empty and vandals came in and destroyed the place. It was then left to my estate to fix it up so it could be sold, and it cost me much more than it should have. In fact, not only did Lou charge me for the supplies to fix the ranch, he also charged me a per hour rate to do it. If Lou had not floated the loan, then none of this would have happened, as the bank would have been the one to deal with them not us.

Another legal aspect that I have strong feelings about is that there be a requirement of proof of legal conservatorship or guardianship and a right to privacy when there is not. In my ALTA files, you can see where my ALTA caseworkers asked my parents repeatedly for proof and copies of my conservatorship, or the "letters of conservatorship" from the court to prove that Lou was my conservator and had a right to know things about me, but there are **no** copies of any sort, so it appears that everything was done verbally, which I do not consider proof!

It seems to me that if someone is going to say they are in charge of all your money and your rights, there should be legal documentation to prove it! And I mean "certified court copies" complete with case and docket numbers, so they can be checked on to make sure that they are real. I also think that this paperwork needs to be updated annually to prove that the status of the conservatorship has not changed during that time. Going over the conservator paperwork at the annual IPP meeting at ALTA would seem like a good time to do it. This would also give the caseworker a chance to ask how the conservatorship is going and ask the client if they want it continued or changed in any way.

I think in this day and age of computers, it's way too easy to fake documentation, and when you are talking about someone's money and their life, it is too important to leave it to a photocopy, especially when it comes to someone's advocate like ALTA is supposed to be. I wonder how many folks are out there whose parents or other "responsible" parties **say** they are the conservator or guardian but have never really been to court. Again, regarding the two kinds of general conservatorships (the estate and the person), I think that there should have to be proof of both sorts annually. Copies should be on file and available to be shown and explained to the client upon request. If these copies are not provided to the appropriate Regional Center within a reasonable time frame (say sixty days from request), then I think the case manager should consider that the conservator no longer has a right to private information without proof and that they say so to the conservator.

If the conservator communicates with the caseworker that they are trying to get the paperwork from the court and there is a delay, then I think that a reasonable extension should be given. To be given the extra time, then I suggest that copies of the documentation being sent to the court requesting the information should also be put in the client's files so that both client and the caseworker know that the "conservator" is actively trying to get the copies from the court. As opposed to in my case where the paperwork was asked for repeatedly but never did not show up, nor was there ever any acknowledgement from Lou regarding ALTA's continued requests for proof of my conservatorship either by phone or letter. He simply ignored all requests as if they never existed.

That is simply not acceptable when someone is in control of your life and money. I believe that Lou was only asked verbally (by phone, perhaps even passed on to him by my mother) for this proof. I think it is important enough to warrant a letter directly to the conservator from the ALTA caseworker so that a hard copy of the request is on file. I think there should be two requests made (one each month), and if no response at all comes, then the ALTA caseworker should notify the conservator that they no longer have a right to the client's personal information. This is a matter of privacy and confidentiality once someone reached the age of eighteen and is no longer a minor. All those years that Lou was my conservator, there was no documented proof of it. ALTA sent copies of my annual reviews to him anyway. But they had no written or legal proof that he actually had a right to get or read them, or even have any information about me after the age of eighteen, and especially later without my permission once I was doing better and things became contentious between us. While I would have certainly given my permission early on for him and my mother to have information about me from ALTA, later when the legal battles began, I would have withdrawn that permission if I could have. This is when ALTA should have demanded written proof from Lou that he was my conservator and had a legal right to my private information. He also exerted control over what I could and couldn't do as far as moving out on my own, but again, there was no proof that he had a legal right to do this.

Regarding the above paragraph. People being given information and control without proof is a giant breach of confidentiality. This could certainly open ALTA or other agencies to enormous legal liability. I most certainly would not want my private information released to anyone that did not have written legal proof that they had a right to it. Under the circumstances, it behooves ALTA and other agencies to make sure they have the right to share private information. While I was under the age of eighteen, my parents of course had the right to my information. But, once I reached eighteen, I don't remember giving consent for my parents to have access to my private information from ALTA. Most likely I did, but just don't remember it. And because Lou told them he was my conservator, that gave him the right to the information, but again, there was no legal documentation ever supplied to prove it. I would have been for the most part fine with the sharing of information when things were going smoothly, but on the other hand, did not want my information shared once things got ugly during the conservatorship battle. And he also did keep me from receiving services and moving out again for a few years when I wanted to live independently, again, though there is no proof that he had the right to do so.

I wonder about those who are under the age of eighteen when they become clients of ALTA, and whose moms and dads had a perfect right to any information about them than as they are minors. But, after they turn eighteen, that would have changed, as they would then be adults and entitled to their privacy if they wished it. If I had had no conservator or guardian, then they would not have had a legal right to information about me without my permission. That could also be a large legal liability, and I would hope that the agencies would demand proof that the parents, or responsible parties of the minor, now have rights to the information about the adult if the adult does not want them to have it anymore.

I know that there is supposed to be an annual meeting held with the Probation Department to check on how the conservatee feels about the status of their conservatorship and conservator. This usually is held in a neutral place with anyone from that person's support team that they want to be there. In my case, this did not happen every year but somewhat sporadically. The first year that I had become unhappy with Lou, I told the probation investigator that I wanted to change things, but when he wrote his report, it did not reflect what I had said. I had told him that I wanted to change the conservatorship of my person, but not my estate. I did not get a copy of it until it had already been sent to and approved by the court, so I could not correct it before the judge saw it. Other people who were at the meeting with me and heard me tell him that I wanted to change things were surprised when the report came back to me after it had been to the judge with no mention of what I had said. I think that after the Probation Department writes the report that it should then be sent back to the conservatee, to make sure it accurately reflects that person's true feeling about the conservator and conservatorship before it is sent to the court for ratification. That way, the probation report does not give the wrong impression of the client's wishes before it's too late and has already been to the court. I realize that this becomes a legal document that goes to the court, and therefore that makes it even more important that this be an accurate reflection of the client's true feelings about their conservator and conservatorship.

I think it would also be vital for the Probation Department (or whoever does the conservatorship review) to also review an annual accounting of the estate. This has to be mandatory, or else the financial abuse could go on for years like it did with me. I think whatever county that you live in, the conservator should have to register to let the local appropriate department know they are there for follow-up on the annual review. There is way too much abuse going on for both disabled adults and seniors. When my parents were investigated by Stanislaus County and told to sell the Greenstone ranch (because they had comingled funds and put the ranch's ownership under the name of the Very Important Pet Motel instead of my name), they simply floated the loan to a private party, comingled our monies yet again, and bought a house in Lodi, which I was not allowed to go to until the very end when they told Bill I had always "had a room there," and there was no further follow-up after that, even though they had just broken the same conservatorship rules they had gotten into trouble with in Stanislaus County. Granted, conservators are not criminals, but they have taken on the responsibility of looking after a vulnerable person. There should be some sort of accountability that goes with that, no matter where they go.

Having discussed the pros and cons of this, I can see a self-funding program whereas someone with an estate like mine would be subject to annual review with the fees paid on a sliding scale dependent on the size of the estate. This means it would not cost the taxpayers extra money to make sure the most vulnerable of the population is looked after fairly. As the baby boomers grow up and get senile, this program could make sure that the wealthiest would have an equal oversight as the poorest. I say this because Social Security makes sure that payees are accountable for the monies spent on their recipients who are disabled, but who looks after the incapacitated well-off?

If the conservatee is unhappy with how things are, then I think that this program should investigate and offer assistance or resources to assist the client to change it if they would like to. I think it would also be a good idea if it had legal resources that could assist the clients or even a just legal resource list we could be referred to. This would be someone we would know we could trust, and in turn, they would have had experience with conservatorships, guardianships, and our population of consumers.

I think that conservatees should also be made aware of the "ex parte" order that is available. I had no idea that my attorney could file a paper that would keep Lou from relocating me on his whim. I would have expressed my unhappiness with the situation much sooner if I had known such a thing existed. Instead, I was terrified to rock the boat or speak what I really thought because I didn't know that I had any sort of protection available. I knew that as my conservator, Lou could move me anywhere he wanted, anytime he wanted, and so I was afraid to say what I really thought because he might move me again. I felt very much under his thumb. After all, he threatened to put me in a locked facility over and over, so who would want to say the wrong thing and find themselves there? As I write this, this brings me to wonder, what *are* the rights of the conservatee? And how does one know what they are? Whose responsibility is it to tell them? Or are they just considered lost souls with no rights? My perception was that I had no rights, and yet with Romana's help, I was able to hire an attorney and get myself free. But before that, I never knew that was an option. So how many others are there now, who are now in the position that I was in and know that they too can do the same thing? Perhaps that is something else that a proper oversight agency can do. Let a conservatee know that there are options available to them and what rights they do have. Granted, not everyone will understand it, but it seems that the effort should be made to educate them.

I mention again that the case of my ex-wife Danielle is a perfect example of everything that went wrong. Her father said he was her guardian, but there was no documented proof, ever. He was taken at his word that this was so. When he pulled her out of ALTA, he would not allow her caseworker to see her or speak with her. This was just a few days after a large meeting in which she told everyone she wanted more space from her parents and more privacy with me. So without legal documentation to back him up, I think that his "word" should not have been enough. If he said she wanted to pull out, then I think a private meeting with just her and her caseworker should have been held at ALTA to see if this is what she really wanted without undue influence from her family.

In our recent research into conservatorships and guardianships, I have come to realize that there is no way he could have been her "guardian" because California State law says that there is *no* guardian for an adult, even one that cannot take care of themselves. Then it is a conservator, not a guardian, and they have to go to court and prove that a guardian is needed, and the extent to which it is needed.

If the family refuses to provide proof that they have the right to interfere with said services, then I think it should be mandatory for ALTA to contact and file an APS (Adult Protective Services) report. The investigation should be conducted by a neutral party and not someone already involved with the family, as happened in Danielle's case. I think that it is unfair to expect someone who has worked with the family to conduct an abuse investigation on one hand, and then come back and work with the family again after that. In Danielle's case, it's hard to know what might have happened. She might have gone along with her parents and agreed to discontinue services, or, she might have taken the opportunity (like she did with Valerie) to really speak her mind and escape from her parents' control. It's sad to think we'll never know what she really wanted in her life because she was never given the chance to say so alone and away from her parents. It's like any other abuse situation; the victim will not speak the truth in the presence of the perpetrator. Especially when you have to go home with them. In fact, in Danielle's case, Valerie Walker offered her home to Danielle if she needed a place to go to get away from her parents. So, if Danielle had had a chance to meet alone with Sally and tell her she didn't want to go home with her parents, then there was an alternative to it. I think it's tragic that Danielle was never given the opportunity to know that that option existed for her. I wonder what sort of placement there might be for a client who wants and needs to escape from a situation like Danielle's. Danielle said that waking up in the hospital after her car accident was her worst nightmare coming true . . . being forever under the control of her father. I tried to help free her, but in the end, they won, and to this day, as far as I know, she is still trapped between the two of them everywhere she goes. She is now in her thirties and seems to have no chance of a life or independence. That is not the life she told me she wanted.

If the person cannot speak or write (as in my case), then this becomes even more important, and a face-to-face meeting with the conservator and with a neutral party present should be mandatory. This neutral party would observe the interaction between the conservator and conservatee to make sure that the relationship is a healthy one and that the client is both listened to and treated with dignity and respect. As someone who was conserved, I would have preferred to meet with my conservator on a quarterly basis. I also think it should have been required for my conservator to see both my home and myself to make sure I was healthy and well and that my home was safe and well cared for.

Perhaps some people are unaware that the conservator is a paid position. As something of an "employee" of the conservatee, I think that to have to meet with the conservatee to make sure that they are happy with the job that the conservator is being paid to do is pretty important. Perhaps a simple evaluation form that the conservatee could fill out would be beneficial for both parties. That way, the conservator would also get feedback on the job that they are doing. I would have liked it also if my conservator (Lou) would have showed me the different things that he did do for me. Perhaps I would have had a better appreciation of his efforts, even if I didn't understand them. That would have certainly made me feel much more connected and aware of my situation. It would have made a huge difference to me if Lou had sat down with me and told me how much my settlement was and how he was spending it. I may not have always understood it well, but I would have appreciated the effort and thought. It would have made me feel more included in my own life.

Perhaps one of the most important things I want to add here is the lack of sheer humanity that Lou had when he handled me and my money. Even when I was most depressed, they never asked or offered to do anything but therapy. It would have made a *huge* difference if they had just packed me up and taken me to Yosemite. They knew how much I loved it there. It would seem common sense that a trip to a place I had loved would be a good thing.

All along the line, Lou never did anything but focus on my money and increasing it, while he slowly killed my soul by excluding me from both knowledge of my money and how it was spent. This caused me much rage and frustration. He refused the communication device and the home I wanted to buy for the sake of "saving my money," which was awarded to me to give me a good quality of life and attempt to make up for what had happened to me. But Lou never once asked what would make *me* happy! He never tried to find out from me what I wanted to do with my money. Everything was about increasing my estate, not my quality of life. The money he gave me monthly was always just enough to get by with perhaps a tiny bit extra. While they took all sorts of trips, I never got to go on any of them. There was plenty of money to pay for someone to be with me on such a trip so that they wouldn't even have had to be fully responsible for me. It was as if the money was the end and be all of everything and I was just an inconvenience. I would much rather have had more say in my money and found other things to do with it besides having it just sit in the bank or in investments. It should have been me and my happiness that was the most important investment. As a result, I grew angrier and angrier as the years went by, and the money was essentially worthless to me because it had no positive effect on my life sitting in a bank collecting interest.

Lou also regularly donated my money to a variety of charities, which I never realized until I got the accountings that showed the different charities and the amounts. But he never asked me if it was all right, or how I felt about it, or if I had a preference for what charities I wanted *my money* spent on. He just took it upon himself to do it on my behalf. This made me angry when I realized that this is what he had been doing. I didn't mind giving to charities, but I wasn't getting much money myself those days and I might have been my own charity. So the bottom line is that I would have liked to have been asked about it and if I wanted my money used for that, and then given an option of what worthwhile charities I might have wanted to donate to.

In comparison, these days, Kellie and I discuss what we are going to use the money for. For instance, we have taken a wonderful trip to a resort in Jamaica, some place I've never been, but was very excited about going to and experiencing. With all the money I have, this was the first trip out of the country that I have ever been on, and that's kinda sad for someone with the amount of money I have had. I could have been doing lots of other things all these years. I really am not that much different now than I was back when this all started. I love nature. And I like seeing new sights. Why did my family, my conservator who is supposed to be looking out for my happiness and well-being, never offer to let me go anywhere?

When Bill Cody was my conservator, I have no doubt that he would have found a way for me to go anywhere I would have wanted to (within reason of course) and if it made me happy, that's all that would have mattered to him. He never said no to anything I wanted, as he said that the money was for me to have a good and enjoyable life.

So, I want family and conservators to know that doing things and using the conservatee's money for good experiences is much more important then it sitting in the bank just collecting interest. I'd rather have the memories and experiences that the money was able to buy, than the larger amounts and life in a stifling little apartment!

I know that there is a difference between having a monthly income that might let someone do more things and a one-time settlement that has to be stretched and made to last. Mine was of the first category. Although, even a settlement can be used to improve the individual's life on an ongoing basis. Ask the person what it is they want. If they can't say, then look at their interests and hobbies and see what can be done to make it a better life for them.

Now, I want to address the issue of Social Security payees. Most of the people I have met and known who were disabled receive Social Security benefits, be it either Social Security on behalf of a parent, or SS Disability Insurance. Many of them have family members who are their payees. Most of them have no idea how much they get from Social Security. Some of them are not even curious as to how much they get. There are others who are controlled by their payees, thinking that because someone is their payee, that also gives them the right to tell them where and how and who they will live with. I know of many cases where the families have so integrated the Social Security funds into their own family budgets that they will tell the individual that they can't move out on their own, when in reality, it is *their* money for their living expenses for wherever they want to live. And many families are also under the mistaken idea that being a payee gives them that right to dictate where and how someone can live that has nothing to do with the finances of it or how much it costs.

There is also a slew of miscellaneous misconceptions that people have about variations of control of a disabled person's rights. For instance, I know of a client who wanted to move in with another client. But her mother had died and written in her will that the client was going to have to always live with her sister and brother-in-law. Now, legally, that is not binding, although there may be monies involved that are only payable *if* she lives with that sibling. However, if she receives SSDI, then that money is not based on her living with her sibling. When she asked her sister if she could move out, the sister said no. And the client has accepted that. I do not know if there is a conservatorship in effect for this person, but that was never given as a reason that she could not move. And I find it very tragic, that just because someone's mother or sibling says they can't move out, that they must lose their dream of living independently when there is no legal basis for it, and when there are wonderful services available to help someone live as independently as possible. How many "normal" people would want to live their lives with their parents or siblings restricting their lives that way? Should they not have the choice and chance to live on their own as well if they can? I was always told that I would never make it on my own, and yet I had and have thrived.

Romana has asked me, that if I only had a choice between living with my parents, or living in a group home, which would I choose? I told her I would have preferred to shoot myself first. But, as much as I didn't like the group home, I would still choose that because at least I would have been living with people who would become my friends. People closer to my own age, and people *not* my parents.

My dream would be for people to live with the least possible control of their lives, and for them to have as much knowledge and control of their money and living situation as possible.

We found this excellent information about conservatorships from the ALTA webpage and are including it here because they really go into excellent details about it.

ALTA California Regional Center
Understanding Conservatorship
A Resource for Families
April 2008

ALTA California Regional Center would like to acknowledge the generosity of Harbor Regional Center for sharing the materials from which this handout was adapted

When your child reaches age eighteen, he/she will be considered an adult under the law and will have the right to make all of the decisions about his/her life that any other adult without a disability can make. This may include, for example, decisions about medical care, a decision to enter into a contract for the purchase of goods or services, or even a decision to marry and have a family. The law does not treat a person differently—limit his/her rights—just because he/she has a developmental disability. Because of your child's disability, however, you may worry about his/her capacity to make some of the decisions that the law allows once a child reaches the age of eighteen and becomes an adult. If you have a serious and longstanding concern about your child's ability to make decisions for him/herself, there is a legal way to limit the decisions that he/she is allowed to make on his/her own. It is called a *conservatorship*. This booklet provides information about the types of conservatorships that are available to residents of California. It describes the ways in which conservatorships limit the ability of a person with a disability to make independent decisions about his/her life. The booklet also suggests alternatives to conservatorship for families who want to protect their son or daughter with a disability while encouraging independence and self-determination.

What is a conservatorship?

Conservatorship is a legal process that gives one person the power to make decisions for another person who is unable to make decisions for himself. The person who obtains the right to make decisions is the *conservator* and the person whose rights are taken away is the *conservatee* or is said to be *conserved*. This is a legal process in which a judge makes the decision about whether or not the person needs to be conserved. California law recognizes three types of conservatorship, but only two of them are relevant to this discussion: *General Conservatorship* and *Limited Conservatorship*. A third type, a Lanterman-Petris-Short (LPS) Conservatorship applies only to a person with serious mental illness. The General Conservatorship may apply to anyone with a disability, while the Limited Conservatorship was created especially to meet the needs of people with a developmental disability. Let's take a closer look at these two types.

General Conservatorship: A General Conservatorship can apply to anyone who has a disability that interferes with decision making. For example, an elderly person with dementia may be subject to a general conservatorship. Under this type of conservatorship, the responsible party may be appointed *conservator of the person* or *conservator of the estate*, or both. The difference between these two types of conservatorships is captured in their titles. Conservatorship *of the person* gives the conservator authority to make decisions about how the person is cared for (e.g., medical care, where and how he or she lives). Conservatorship *of the estate* relates to decisions about the person's money and property. Before a court will appoint someone a conservator of the person, the party requesting the conservatorship must demonstrate to the court that the proposed conservatee is unable to properly provide for his or her own needs related to food, clothing or shelter, and health care. Similarly, to be appointed conservator of the estate, a party must demonstrate that the person is unable to manage his or her personal finances, or would be vulnerable to fraud or to "undue influence" of another who may not have the best interest of the person as a primary concern.

Limited Conservatorship: A Limited Conservatorship applies only to adults with a developmental disability, as defined in California law. When petitioning for a conservatorship for a person with a developmental disability, the petition must be for a limited conservatorship, although the judge has the right to award a General Conservatorship. The protection is "limited" in that the conservator is given authority to make decisions only in areas where the court believes the disabled person needs help. Therefore, the judge must make a separate decision about each of the following seven rights:

- The right to determine where and with whom he or she lives

- The right of access to his or her confidential (educational, medical, etc.) records
- The right to marry
- The right to enter into a contract
- The right to consent to medical treatment
- The right to have social or sexual contacts
- The right to make decisions about his or her education.

A Limited Conservatorship can give the conserved person a higher degree of control by allowing him to make some, but not all, decisions about his life. It encourages the person to be independent and engage in self-direction to the extent that he is able. Neither form of conservatorship can be used to control behavior or unduly restrict lifestyle choices.

Who can be the conservator?

When a regional center client is conserved, it is most often a parent or a sibling who becomes the conservator. There is no rule that says a conservator must be a relative, but it should be someone in whom the family has a great deal of trust. There are professional conservators who will take on this role for a fee, but selecting a person for this role is itself a challenging task. Institutions such as the Department of Developmental Services or the public guardian's office may also serve as conservator for a person who has no one else in his or her life who could effectively play this role.

If you are considering asking one of your other children to become conservator for his or her sibling with a disability, we encourage you to have a full discussion about this well before it is time for him or her to take this step. This type of arrangement works well for some families, but being a conservator brings with it significant responsibilities over a long period of time. You will want to know that the sibling who is to take on this role understands it fully and accepts it willingly.

What do I need to think about when making a decision about a conservatorship?

If you are considering seeking a conservatorship for your son or daughter, we encourage you to think about the following questions:

1) *Do people who have provided support or otherwise worked with our son or daughter recommend a conservatorship?* Sometimes someone outside of your family has been in a position to observe your child extensively and may have information that can be helpful in your decision making. Talk to your ACRC counselor, your child's teachers, job coach, or others who provide him with support and ask them for their opinion about your child's ability to make decisions in specific areas. They may have observed a level of independence in certain areas that you yourself have not seen in your child.

2) *Can we gain decision-making powers in some areas through means other than a court-appointed conservatorship?* There are alternatives to conservatorship for parents concerned about their disabled child's future welfare. For example, the use of the "Assignment of Educational Decision Making" may provide an effective way for you to continue involvement in your child's education and health care. This and other possible strategies are discussed below.

3) *Can we address our concerns in the IPP through the planning team process?* Your ACRC Service Coordinator or the service providers who work with your son or daughter may be able to help you develop ways to address your concerns, particularly about issues such as social and sexual relationships and entering contracts.

4) *If we decide to pursue a conservatorship, what are the areas in which we really believe he needs our help and in what areas can we give him more of a role in decision making?* The Limited Conservatorship was developed specifically for people with developmental disabilities to allow them to participate in decision making to the extent appropriate. For example, although a person may not have the judgment necessary to consent to a complex medical procedure, he may, simply with your guidance and support, be able to decide where and with whom he wants to live.

What are some alternatives to conservatorship?

Obtaining a conservatorship is a legal process that takes some time and has associated financial costs. In addition, most people find they need to hire a lawyer to complete the process. A conservatorship is a useful and appropriate tool for many families who want assurance that someone will be there for their disabled son or daughter after they are gone. At the same time, it is not the only way for parents to deal with their concerns about their child's future. Before seeking a conservatorship, families should realistically evaluate their child's capacity to make appropriate decisions in each of the seven areas, either independently or with support. They should also investigate other possible ways to ensure their child's welfare while allowing him to retain his civil rights.

Over the years, we have found that if families discuss issues of concern with their regional center counselor or other professionals, they are often able to create reasonable alternatives that balance their need to protect their child against the child's right to self-determination and desire for independence.

Below we give some examples of strategies that families have used successfully to help their adult sons and daughters participate in decision making about their lives while ensuring that they are safe from harm and exploitation.

Educational Decisions: Your child with a disability is likely to remain in a public school program until he is twenty-one years of age. When he reaches the age of eighteen, however, all educational decision-making authority transfers from you to him unless he has been determined incompetent under California law. You may have become accustomed to close collaboration with the school district in planning for your child's future and would like that to continue that involvement. There is a way for you to continue being involved after your child turns eighteen that is effective and not as costly or complicated as seeking a conservatorship. You may have your son or daughter sign an "Assignment of Educational Decision Making," giving consent for your continued involvement in his educational program. When signed, this form gives you the right to make a variety of decisions about his education and transition from school. (You should renew this document each year that your child remains in school.) We have included a sample of this document at the end of this booklet. It was taken from the web site of Protection and Advocacy, Inc, California, www.paica. org. We have found that school personnel are often unfamiliar with this document, so you may need to refer officials from your child's school to the PAI website.

Social and Sexual Contacts: Some families consider becoming conservator of their children because they have concerns about social relationships and sexual contacts that their children may become involved in as they enter adulthood. Sometimes parents believe that their son or daughter will be unable to safely and effectively handle the complex issues and potential consequences of intimate relationships.

Many people with a developmental disability have intimate relationships, and some even marry. As an alternative to pursuing a conservatorship, you may wish to talk to your ACRC Service Coordinator about programs that are available through the regional center to help young adults learn about dating, sexuality, and developing healthy social relationships. Your counselor can also share with you ways these matters have been handled by other families. The ACRC Kelso Library is another place where you can find a variety of books, videos, and DVDs dealing with these subjects.

You also have an important role to play by having ongoing open discussions with your child about relationships. Thoughtful discussion, effective planning, and appropriate education can give him a sound basis for dealing with interpersonal situations that arise. ACRC professionals and services providers who work with your child can give you suggestions for how to structure these discussions.

Medical Consent: Some families seek a conservatorship so they will have the right to consent to medical care to ensure their son or daughter receives recommended preventive care or necessary medical procedures. This may not be necessary if you maintain collaborative relationships with the medical professionals who treat your child. Maintaining these relationships will help smooth the way for your continued involvement as your child makes his transition to adulthood so that, with his or her consent, you can continue to be involved in decision making about his health care.

Financial Agreements and Contracts: Sometimes families believe they need a conservatorship to prevent their child from entering into legal agreements (for credit cards, cell phones, etc.) that are exploitive or that he may not be financially able to honor. The first strategy for addressing this concern is to help your child develop the tools he will need to be a smart consumer. You can begin by talking to him about things such as offers he may receive in the mail or on email and the consequences of signing a document without first discussing it with you or another trusted adult. You can also encourage your child's school to include budgeting and money management as a goal on his IEP.

If you decide that your child will always need help managing his money, you can become or arrange for someone else to become his "representative payee." This is a relative or trusted friend, or payee service agency who will receive his Supplemental Security Income (SSI) to use on his behalf. More information about a representative payee is available on the web at http://www.ssa.gov/pubs/10076.html.

If your child were to enter into a contract that you believe he doesn't understand or that he will be unable to honor, you may want to talk with your ACRC service coordinator about requesting a referral to the Office of Clients Rights Advocacy for assistance in securing a reversal of a contract or dismissal of a legal action intended to enforce a contract.

If I seek a conservatorship, does the regional center get involved?

If you choose to seek a Limited Conservatorship for your son or daughter who is a regional center client, we will be asked by the court to provide a report with our opinion about his or her need for a conservator in each of the seven areas. His or her service coordinator will review the IPP, current psychological and medical evaluations, and other assessments or service provider reports that describe current functioning. If necessary, the service coordinator may arrange for additional evaluations. After gathering all of the necessary information, the counselor will write the report and include the regional center's recommendations in each area. Because we know that families almost always take this action because of their concern for the health and safety of their adult child with a disability, ALTA California Regional Center usually supports the families' decisions in these matters. In some circumstances, we may disagree that the consumer is in need of a conservator or that the conservatorship should extend to all of the areas requested by the family, and we will give our rationale for our views to the family and the court. Our findings and recommendations are not binding on the court, however.

Where can I get more information about conservatorships?

If you are just beginning to think about conservatorships, you may find it very helpful to discuss the concept with an attorney familiar with the law governing conservatorships and the steps involved in obtaining one. If, after considering the alternatives, you believe that obtaining a conservatorship is the best thing for your son or daughter and your family, we encourage you to speak with your regional center service coordinator. He or she may suggest a meeting with an attorney who can help you better understand. Your service coordinator can also direct you to specific publications in the ACRC Kelso Library where you will find a variety of books, videos, and brochures on conservatorships and how to obtain one.

A Final Note . . . At ALTA California Regional Center, we know that many families have questions about how to promote their young adult's independence while continuing to protect them from potential harm. Conservatorship is one way to shelter them from the consequences of poor decision making, And this is why we want to make sure that family members are well-informed about this legal alternative. We also know, however, that conservatorship can limit an adult's freedom and independence unnecessarily. ALTA California Regional Center is committed to promoting a strong, ongoing relationship between people with developmental disabilities and their family members while helping our adult clients live more productive, independent lives. We encourage you to seriously consider every alternative to conservatorship before proceeding with this approach, and we will provide you with all of the support and guidance needed to help you make the best decision for your unique circumstances.

ASSIGNMENT OF EDUCATIONAL DECISIONMAKING AUTHORITY
California Education Code Section 56041.5

I, _____, having reached the age of eighteen years, having never been determined to be incompetent for any purpose by a court of competent jurisdiction, and having received, at the age of majority, all educational decision making authority pursuant to California Education Code Section 56041.5, hereby authorize my parent, _____, to make any and all decisions for me regarding my entitlement to a Free Appropriate Public Special Education. Such authority shall include, but is not limited to:

1. Filing complaints with any public agency, such as the California Department of Education and U.S. Department of Education, Office for Civil Rights;
2. Initiating and pursuing special education due process proceedings pursuant to Cal. Education Code Sec. 56500, et seq. and any judicial appeals thereof;
3. Attending IEP meetings and due process mediations and predue process mediations and signing IEP documents and mediation agreements with the same legal effect and authority as I would have absent this assignment;

4. Authorizing or refusing to authorize assessments, services, or placements;
5. Obtaining copies of any of my educational, psychological, medical, behavioral, or juvenile justice records, or any other materials and information related in any way to my special education, related services, supplementary aids and services, or transition services;
6. Receiving information orally from any individual or agency (public or private) regarding my special education rights or services;
7. Exercising any other right or action on my behalf concerning my education with the same authority as I would have absent this assignment.

A photocopy or facsimile of this document shall have the same effect as the original.

Dated: _____

Source: http://www.paica. org/pubs/505001.htm#_Toc122236172

Chapter 17

Sharing What I've Learned
(My thoughts on group homes and
institutionalized living)

Over the years, I have lived in a variety of situations. Some private, with my family, and a variety of group homes that were both nonindependent and semi-independent. At the last place that I was, there was an apartment that was attached to the group home, and I lived there with a roommate. We got along all right most of the time. We did have some differences of opinion of course. But we had our own kitchen and were able to shop and cook as we wanted, which was not too bad. It was still rather oppressive, however. I then finally moved out on my own after a lot of wrangling with the staff over what they wanted me to do. I would have liked to have moved out much sooner, but my parents wouldn't let me, and that frustrated me a lot. I had lived on my own in the past till my parents brought me to live with them after I was in Davis. Granted, I had some difficulties, but nothing that couldn't be worked out with a good support system.

Romana and I have talked about my past experiences in the variety of places that I have lived. She has asked me to share my insight about living in a nonindependent situation and what things I have seen and felt during those years that might be able to help others have a higher quality of life. I can say that I have never lived in a totally institutionalized setting, but I have lived in some group homes that were very structured. Lou would use the threat of sending me to a "locked facility" enough for me to think about what it would be like, and the thought terrified me. So I did my best to behave in spite of my anger difficulties. And I learned to "kiss ass" to get by with the staff to get out of that last place. We even developed a special sign for it, and when I'd start to get mad at them, if Romana was around, she'd flash that sign at me and I knew I better calm down and behave and not argue, even if I knew I was right and they were wrong. That didn't matter; submitting to them is all that would get me out of there.

While living in a group home, not being able to have the choice to go out or not go out with the group was my biggest frustration. My suggestion would be that when possible, a staff member stay behind so residents would have the option of going out on group outings or not. Not being able to choose if I wanted to go out or not made me feel stupid and childlike and not at all like an adult. I never enjoyed the lectures about why I *had* to go out whether I wanted to or not. Living in the formal group home was the most difficult part because we were all herded together with few choices as to food or roommates or options of how we wanted to spend our time. For the most part, we all had to do whatever the staff told us to do and that was very frustrating. That made me feel like a marionette and not liking how they controlled my strings. And again, it made me feel very stupid and *not* like an adult learning independence.

My perspective is that my folks just wanted me "store housed" someplace where they didn't have to think about how I was doing, just that I was being "looked after." It felt like it didn't matter how happy I was there, just that I was being taken care of by someone. While I would have preferred to have my own life and live independently.

Another thing that makes a bigger difference than most folks would think about is food. Some places don't give the residents any choice as to what they are going to eat. The staff decides and we eat it whether we like it or not. Some good options would have been allowing the residents to come up with things that we chose to eat as a group for our meals. I can understand that in a group home setting, there do need to be some decisions about food and what folks are going to eat. But a compromise would be letting the residents choose and vote on what sort of foods they want to eat. For those folks that are more disabled or nonverbal, a poster with different pictures of food that they could point to would be a way to offer them a choice that they normally wouldn't get. As someone who has had to live with no choices allowed, even what seems to most folks as a small choice can be a big one. Having a say in what you eat can make a big difference in making you feel like you count as an individual. I think that the staff in the institutions have no idea how important that sort of thing can be. Eating foods that you like and choose are healthier for you because you're more likely to eat it, and funny as it sounds, it really does help your self-esteem to be able to eat something that you have chosen to eat. For instance, in a choice between milk and juice, perhaps the person would like both!

Being able to choose roommates is also a big step toward being empowered. At one time, I had a roommate who was a complete slob. I was a real neat freak and he wasn't. This caused us both stress and multiple disagreements. I knew that this particular living situation was temporary, so I think I was able to handle it better. If it had been a long-term or permanent situation, then because I didn't choose him as a roommate of my own, I would have had a much harder time as well. I think that it would be very empowering to give residents a choice as to whom they want to room with. Or perhaps roommates have gotten bored with each other and want to switch rooms out. What I am saying, again, is that being given the ability to make a choice is as important as either making or not making a choice to change a situation. It is the option of having the choice to make that is the important part. Just because folks are disabled does **not** mean that they don't have preferences. Taking the choices away makes us all robots. I realize that the staff doesn't necessarily do this to be mean, most of it is done in the name of efficiency, but leaves quality of life in the toilet.

Another difference, again may seem trivial to others but would have made a difference to me, was the signing-out process. When Romana would come see me, she had to sign me out as though I was not responsible enough to sign myself out, and also made me feel like I was a prisoner who was being transferred, as opposed to my signing myself out that I was going with her. This may not seem like a big difference, and it's not really, but when it's you being shuffled around, there is a difference in **my** signing myself out to go somewhere and someone else signing me out like a child to go somewhere. One makes you feel more like an adult, the other doesn't. I can see in some situations where it is appropriate for someone to be signed out, but perhaps in that case both can sign out. That way, both the requirement of having the "responsible" person sign the person out is met, and the individual remains an adult by signing themselves out as well. Even if it's just making a mark to represent themselves. Again, seems like a small difference, but I would not have felt so stupid and it would have made me feel more responsible for myself to sign myself out.

Some folks move into a group home and never want to move out. They like the stability, the routines, and the camaraderie of it. For some folks, that's as independent as they ever want to be.

Some of them just want to get out of their parents' home and they consider the group home their comfort level of independence. Some won't ever master the skills needed to move out on their own. Others are more like me and are there only to get stabilized and learn whatever skills they may need to live independently. Whichever the choice is, I think it's best if the individual can choose for themselves. As for those who can't learn the skills but still want to move out, then again, the least confining is the best way to go I think. Perhaps a private roommate situation would allow both extra support for living independently and not have the restrictions of a group home. I had one like that when I very first moved out of the last group home. My folks paid for me to have a roommate, and he helped me look after things and get myself situated. Once I had been living on my own for a while, then I didn't need his help anymore, and I was able to live totally alone with the help of my support system.

There are lots of options out there, and the best way to go is to get as much input from the individual as possible so that they feel they are included in the decision-making process, and that will help them feel more independent. The more choices that they can make in regards to their living situation, the better!

Chapter 18

Predators of the Disabled
(How loneliness and desperation
can let the predator in)

The next subject that I want to address is the predator of the disabled. I wrote earlier about the woman who picked me up and moved in with me. I have since learned that there is an evil type of person who knows where the disabled go to, and in particular, look for lonely people and then make "friends" with them and then manipulate them for as much money or other things as possible. Disabled folks (like the rest of us) just want to fit in, and they will go to great lengths to try to do this. Even if that means their new "friend" is not good for them or is taking advantage of them. This can be especially true of men and sex. It is harder for many disabled men to find women to meet their physical needs, and female predators know this and take as much advantage of it as possible. The men will do almost anything for sex, including putting up with some pretty awful treatment and manipulation, and giving away lots of money, sometimes money they cannot afford.

This happened to me, to some extent, and to others that I know of to a much larger extent. In fact, I know of two men who owned a home and there was a woman who had managed to involve herself with both of them, playing them each against the other. She had taken financial advantage of them to the degree where the county has had to intervene and have them both conserved. Both the person (their rights) and their estate (their money). So they have both lost the control they had of their lives because of this. One of them was sent to a group home in another town a couple hours away where he is quite miserable. He hates it there and has lost all contact with the friends that he had here. The other was also sent to a group home in another town as well. His father became sick and he was just able to make it home before his father died due to the intervention of his ILS worker, not the county guardian. He wanted to stay with his mom, but the guardian did not let him move home with her and he was sent back to the group home. Since he had all his rights taken away, neither he nor his mother have any say where he actually lives now. I find that just awful. So you can see to the degree that the predator has destroyed their lives. Perhaps in time he will be able to show he can make good decisions again and move in with his mother.

I suppose that I find this situation even more distressing because this could have been me permanently. As my conservator, Lou did exactly the same thing to me. As opposed to Bill, who came and talked with me about things and listened to me. But the predator doesn't care about what happens to the individual, only getting as much as they can out of the disabled person before they get caught or the money is cut off.

It bears mentioning that women are often as venerable as men are, and sometimes find themselves in even more danger because the man can hurt them physically, and that is certainly more apt to happen with a male predator than a female. The female predator will most often use her sexuality and feminine wiles to control the man, but the male predator will tend to use control and bullying and even the threat of physical force or harm to control the disabled female.

A sure sign that things are not going right is when the predator begins to isolate the disabled person, chasing their friends and support away. This separates them and leaves them alone from being protected by their friends. This makes it easier for them to be hurt in a variety of ways and no one is aware of it. The predator will also often tell the disabled person that whatever it is, is their "secret" and to not tell anyone else about it. This is a sure sign that something is not right.

There was also another situation that came up with me just as Bill was taking over as my conservator. The staff at MORE workshop knew I had an interest in photography, and the son of two of the staff members was a professional photographer. They introduced us and we got along quite well. The idea was that I would be an assistant to him and learn more about photography on an enhanced professional level.

In my opinion. however, he wasn't that good of a photographer. By that I mean he didn't seem to have a very good eye. I wasn't terribly impressed by his artistic skills, but he did know how the equipment worked and I wanted to learn more about that. Somewhere along the line, he mentioned that he needed some financing to expand his business and get new equipment.

Back then I used to talk somewhat inappropriately about how much money I had (or thought I had), and I must have mentioned it to him because he asked to borrow $2,000 from me. The deal was that I would then be a partner with him in the photography business. I had him fax the contract to Romana at Choices. I hadn't told her about the loan yet, but this was my way of letting her know. The first thing that she did was to call Bill. I had already given the photographer the money at this point, however. And the contract "payment" was supposed to be $100 a month for eighteen months, but the one he sent was only for a year. Which, of course, doesn't add up to $2000, as it is $800 short. It would be accurate to say that both Bill and Romana were rather upset by this. They were not mad at me; they knew how generous I could be, but they were extremely upset at the photographer for taking advantage of me, especially since the contract didn't add up to pay back what had been borrowed. Shortly after the loan, he had a nervous breakdown and I didn't see him anymore. So much for being a "business partner." He by then had made only two payments back to me. We tried to reach him but he wasn't returning our calls. So, Bill and I went to MORE workshop where his father worked so that Bill could talk to his dad about getting my money back. The man got extremely angry with me and started yelling at both Bill and I. He said that I had caused his son's nervous breakdown by "bugging" him about paying the money back when he didn't have an income to pay it back with. He said it was my entire fault in the first place for offering his son the loan. Excuse *me*? Who is the disabled person here? Besides that, he *asked* for the loan! I was in shock because this man and I had always gotten along very well in the past, and I was hurt and angry at how he was treating me and blaming me for his son's illness.

He was also enraged at us for involving him. But since he had been the one to introduce us, it did seem like some responsibility should lay with him. He told Bill that his son had borrowed money from another family member and not paid him back either. So in the end, I didn't get my money back, but I did learn a good lesson. And that was to not loan money to people I don't know well enough to trust. And to try and get some sort of collateral if possible. In retrospect, I should have asked for some of the photography equipment as collateral. Even if I didn't use it, I might have been able to sell it. In the end, I do believe in karma and that it will come full circle. He's in a mental institution and I'm doing much better thank you very much!

One of the other things I'd like to touch on briefly is how some of the differing disabilities can also be manipulated. One of them is using the fact that someone might not understand what is going on, but will act as if they do. And the individual with the "agenda" will **know** this but ignore it on purpose so that they can get what they want and then say "well I asked them and they said yes," knowing full well that the individual did **not** understand. And there is also the difficulty with language and words. Most people don't want someone to know they didn't understand something said (a word for instance), and they also will just go along with it rather then expose their ignorance of the word or concept. The individual they are talking with may or may not be aware of this. It can be embarrassing to ask someone, "Did you understand what I meant by that?" This can however give the disabled person a chance to "save face" and say "no, not quite." The predator is of course less likely to do this as they don't want to know that the person didn't understand them. It does tend to be easier to manipulate some of the developmentally disabled because they don't expect to be taken advantage of. They tend to take people more at face value. They also tend to be much more trusting of people. I'd say they go along with things they don't quite understand and hope for the best. Again, this is exactly the sort of situation that the predators look for. They can tell if someone didn't realize that their story didn't quite add up and will use that lack of understanding to exploit them in whatever manner they want. The predator of the disabled is a master of manipulation, and it's up to all of us to keep an eye on those of us in our community less fortunate in their understanding of life.

I would suggest that friends and family do their best to be aware of what is going on in their loved one's life. And please, for their sake, don't give up even when it seems impossible. During the roughest times, Romana, Bill, and Bruce didn't give up on me, and I'm eternally glad that they didn't!

Chapter 19

Services for the Disabled
(What's available and drawbacks to beware of)

PART ONE
OUR PERSPECTIVE

This chapter is broken up into two parts. The first part is a narrative about the different agencies that we are aware of, our perceptions, interaction with them, and to some degree, our opinions on them.

The second part will be information taken from the Web sites of the agencies that we mention and in their own words with no comments from us about them.

Services for the disabled vary worldwide. In the United States, there are many programs available. I am currently unaware of what sort of assistance is obtainable in other countries. Mostly I know about California since that is where I live. In the second part of this chapter, we have tried to import information directly from the Web sites of the agencies that we will write about here; that way, they are speaking in their own words about the services that they provide.

I do know that there is an international grass roots self-advocacy group called "People First." The name comes from the idea that while they may have some disabilities, they are *people first.* They may have the information about services for the disabled in your area. They are an excellent resource of all sorts of information, and they are also very strong watchdogs for legislation that impacts the disabled as well as influential lobbyists politically. They are good at writing petitions and holding demonstrations to make sure the rights of the disabled are not overlooked. Every year, they gather here in the USA to hold a national conference that has a wide variety of workshops and classes to learn from and participate in. This is a great place to meet people and learn about your rights. They will also teach you how to speak out for yourself and your rights. If you're not used to standing up for yourself, then People First will help you learn how to do it. But it's not easy to learn to stand up for yourself, and it seems that there will always be someone telling that you can't do something that *they* think you can't.

We also have to be reasonable about what we can do. We all have limitations and have to learn to live with some of them. For instance, I would have loved to have still been a veterinarian. But because of my accident, my brain simply wouldn't work well enough for me to go to school and handle all that the job would have demanded of me. So instead, I have my own pets and take care of them. It's not the same thing, but I am happy with my life as it has evolved, and that includes my pets. Sometimes the hardest thing is to accept your limits and live with them. The flip side of that is listening to reasonable folks who see something that they think you can change, even when you are afraid to. For instance, I was terrified to try and change my conservator, and Romana had to really talk me into trying to do it. In regards to that, she believed it could be done more than I did at the time. Finding my wonderful wife was the same way. I was convinced that no one would ever love me because I couldn't speak. Romana wouldn't let that be a reason for me not to try, however. She said I could communicate and that the right person would love me. And she was right then, too! So I am glad that I listened to her and tried even though I didn't agree with her at the time.

You have to make sure that the person giving you advice really does have your best interests at heart and not some sort of other motive. You need to make sure the person is trustworthy though and is not trying to get you to do something that may be good for them but not for you. You need to make sure that you are looking at the *big picture*. And you need to think with your mind, not just your emotions. To be frank, money and sex seem to be the two biggest things that people manipulate others to gain. So if someone wants either of those things from you to "help" you, then they are *not* looking out for your best interests. Find someone who doesn't want anything from you but for you to be happy, and most likely you can trust them. Trusting people who have been in your life and shown you that they don't want something from you is also a good key to knowing that they desire only good things for you.

There are times to accept your limitations and times not to. God will open those doors that are supposed to, but you have to do your part and try.

As far as government services, let's talk about the financial ones first. There is Social Security programs: SSA and/or SSDI. You can almost always count on being turned down the first time you apply unless the disability is **very** severe. Sometimes you can get it overturned yourself, and other times you will need an attorney to help you. In general, these days it takes a couple of years. So you have to have a lot of determination and persistence. And be able to fill out massive amounts of paperwork over and over and over.

Once you get on SSA/SSDI, that endless stream of paperwork will continue. Don't expect too much logic out of the system either, nor for it to be friendly or helpful. The bureaucracy is just too big. They don't really mean to be frustrating, they just are. You'll need lots of patience. There are many rules to keeping one's SSDI income. In particular to SSDI (Social Security Disability Insurance) are the stricter financial rules. One of them is to live in a state of poverty to stay on the program. You can't save more than $2,000 or you can be cut off. You can't be married to someone with any sort of income that is above the very minimum. You can do it with a roommate, but you can't do it with a spouse if they make any sort of money. Nor can you have any sort of legal connections. No shared bank accounts or property (such as both your names on a car).

The amount that Social Security pays is rarely enough for an individual to live on independently. Almost everyone that I know of on it has to have a roommate. The amount of SSDI does not keep up with the cost of living. It's a system that often keeps couples from being together legally. It would seem to us that the government could at least move the financial bar up for assistance from spouses if they are not going to pay more as the price of living increases.

While we are talking about SSA and SSI, it behooves us to mention again the situation of those that have "payees" and what that does and doesn't mean. Many of the folks whose parents are their payees think that means that it is the same as them being their conservator. And the parents sometimes think the same thing! Some parents think that means that any and **all** monies that the individual gets (be it from Social Security, ALTA, or work) goes to them. Often the parents also think this gives them the right to tell their adult children how to live their lives, including whether they can move out on their own or not. This certainly puts stress on the individual that wants to move out on their own. In many cases (as we have discussed before), family members have been using that SSA/SSI money in their own budgets for a considerable time. When the disabled person reaches adulthood and wants to move out on their own, this is often an obstacle. The family has been using that money for so long that it is wrapped

SERVICES FOR THE DISABLED

up in the family budget. I know of a case where an ALTA caseworker had to step in and give the family a six-month notice that ALTA was going to become the payee, and the family had best figure out a way to deal with it. Otherwise the client who wanted to live on his own in town (instead of way out in the country where his family lived) would most likely never have been able to move. He was not strong enough to do it himself. He did ask his ALTA caseworker for help, but I think there are many situations where the client is not strong enough to do even that. Or they don't want to cause a hardship for their family and hence, sacrifice their own desires for the sake of their family, and that is an unfair situation to put anyone in. "If you leave, we can't pay our bills." I'd call that emotional blackmail. Social Security rules are that the money is supposed to be used for the individual, **not** the family. But few clients realize this. And many of the families are not eager to let it be known. It is a vicious circle.

My suggestion is that the less the family members are payees, the better. Many folks seem to think that no one will look out for someone as well as a family member. I can tell you from firsthand experience that that is **not** necessarily the case! In my circumstance, my family took advantage of being both my payee and my conservator. I am sure I would have been much better off if a stranger had been my payee. At least then the bureaucrats would have looked closer at my situation I think, rather then expecting that my parents would never do anything wrong with my money. This also caused stress and disharmony between my siblings and me. My sister Stephanie in particular became very upset with me for trying to take control of my finances and life back from Lou. And once I began fighting him legally for my freedom, then I became essentially an outcast from my family. This made me very sad and frustrated. They knew Lou's side of the story and never even came to see or talk with me about my side. To this day, Stephanie still thinks that Lou is the greatest dad ever . . . while I can see he was good at one time, until greed got in the way. My mother of course thinks the same thing as Stephanie, but we may just have to agree to disagree on this.

There are also local state programs that offer help. I don't know much about them other than in California. I know for instance that here we also have IHSS (In-Home Support Services). This is a program that pays people to help seniors and people with disabilities living in their own homes. An IHSS worker may do shopping that you can't do, take you to the doctors, cook, and/or clean as well. It all depends on what the individual's disability and need is. The hours of services will also vary depending on the requirement. Here in California, we worked for many years to get the pay at above minimum wage so that we would have a higher quality of people taking care of the most vulnerable of our population. Before there were many cases of IHSS workers who weren't making enough to live on, so they "helped themselves" to some of the disabled and seniors' assets or property. It was a matter of the less fortunate taking advantage of the weaker members of society.

The IHSS system that I personally know the most about would be the one in El Dorado County. There are no real qualifications to be hired other than wanting to do the job. There is a very small pool of folks who do the work up there, and most often the individual who needs the services will need to find their own worker. This can also be a family member or friend. Many of the people who need IHSS workers place ads and interview the folks who will help them. The pitfall to that is that they are forced to have a variety of people in their home that may not be completely trustworthy. And it seems down right dangerous to me to have strangers coming into the home of a frail elderly individual. Part of the point is to protect the weaker in our society, not expose them to danger. I would have grave concerns if this was a family member of mine who had to go through this process without someone else there to help. I don't quite know what the answer is, but the current setup is not the best idea for the public safety of our disabled and elderly.

There was a time when Romana was an IHSS worker for a paraplegic man. Her experience was that she answered his ad in the local "pennysaver." She then went out to meet him at his home for an interview. There was no one else present but the two of them. Looking back at it, this could have been a dangerous situation for both of them. She says that she should have at least called IHSS to make sure he really *was* registered with IHSS and not some dangerous crackpot. And he should have had someone there as well, as she could have been the dangerous crackpot now in this defenseless man's home. They were both exposed to danger under that situation.

So, I suppose that a good suggestion would be that if you are going to answer an ad for IHSS, that you get their name and phone number and call IHSS to make sure they really are on the IHSS program. Then make an appointment to meet the person and try to have someone from IHSS there. That would make sure that everyone is safe. We also think that the very best situation would be to have the first meeting at the IHSS offices; that way the perspective employee wouldn't know the individual's address until they were determined to be a safe person.

In many cases, it is a family member who does the IHSS work. This can be good and bad. On the one hand, they know the individual, but on the other, it does bring money into the relationship. For instance, we still feel that this was a part of why the Alexanders took Danielle back. Her mother was getting many hours to look after her. When we married and I began to look after Danielle and didn't want nor need to be paid for it, her mother lost that decent-sized bit of income. Danielle had heard them talking about the loss of this income as a difficulty for them. And this was a reason her parents wanted us to live with them. Once Danielle was living back at home with them, her mother started getting paid for the IHSS hours again. So in that case, having her parents dependent on the IHSS monies was **not** a good thing. And this is something to think about if someone is considering having a family member do the IHSS work for them.

Again, in Danielle's case, while technically Mrs. Alexander was Danielle's "employee," Danielle had no idea of that or of her rights in regards to that. This blurs the relationship between them as far as parent and worker. It can be a good thing if done right, but not so good if someone is prone to dominate the situation. It also can isolate the individual. Having someone from the outside come in can be a very good thing and expose the person to more variety. Having an even remotely controlling parent can exclude others from the person's life. And variety is a good thing. If it were I, I would like to have a new person to meet and talk to and do things with. If I lived with my parents, I'd see enough of them as it was. And it also would make me feel a lot more independent to have someone working for me that was not my parent. And it would also be one less person telling me what to do. Another benefit of having an outside person come in would be as in the case of Danielle. If someone from the outside had come in on a regular basis, then they would have seen Mr. Alexander's treatment of her. And as a mandated reporter, perhaps Mr. Alexander would have at least had to be on better behavior, and there might have been another pair of eyes to report some of the things going on. Which is most likely why they didn't want someone else to come in. Well, that and the money of course.

We think that around the age of twenty-one (depending on the individual) is a good age to change from having your parent be your IHSS worker to having an outside individual. Parents can always be a backup if needed. As for elderly folks, I think it should be much the same way. The problem of course is finding a good quality, reliable, and compassionate person to help. I think it would be a more rewarding experience to have outside individuals involved as much as possible. If I were an elderly person who needed assistance, I think I'd rather have someone other than my daughter assisting me with my most personal needs. That would also allow her to be my daughter and not my caregiver. I realize that in many situations, this is not a possibility, as finding the right individual can be a real challenge. I do also understand that in many cases, the children do end up being the parents' caregiver. And I would hope that if there were no one else to look after me, that my child would love me enough to help.

Next there is the Housing Choice Voucher Program (HCVP) (formerly known as the Sec 8 program). This is a national program run by HUD (US Department of Housing and Urban Development) that helps out low-income people to be able to afford to live in their own place. There are many financial restrictions on this program as well. First off, you of course have to be low income. Currently, it is one person can't earn more than $23,500 annually, two persons $26,900. This goes up roughly $3,000 more per person. You can't have anyone helping you to pay your rent. The HCV Program has to inspect and approve of the place before you can move into it. Or if you are living someplace already when you are finally approved for it, they will have to inspect it to see if you can stay there, or you will need to move someplace that does accept the HCV Program. The landlord also has to agree to accept the Voucher Program. Many landlords don't like dealing with people on the program because they don't like the bureaucracy telling them what they can and can't do. Some "slum lords" also don't want to have to bring their property up to "code" or the standards of the HVC Program. There is also annual paperwork and annual inspections. The way that HVC Program works is that based on your income, you pay part of the rent and HVC Program pays the rest of it. The amounts depend on the place you are living, people living with you, and your income. The tenant pays roughly 30 percent of their income to the landlord. There are restrictions on long-term visitors as well.

Currently, the HVC Program has (like many other programs) suffered from budget cuts. So the waiting list (at least in El Dorado County) has been closed for several years. In February of 2008, the list was opened for the first time since 2002 for some fourteen days. They got some one thousand four hundred applications in those fourteen days. There are people currently still on the waiting list from 1998. That is a darned long time to wait. So it's not anything that folks can even count on these days if they don't have a voucher for the program yet. With more cuts on the horizon, who knows how long it may take to get on it?

Regional Centers

Here in California, we have "Regional Centers" that assist the developmentally disabled with a variety of services. They are under the jurisdiction of the California Department of Developmental Disabilities. You have to have been diagnosed with a disability that occurred before the age of twenty-one in order to be eligible. There is an evaluation process that you go through, and if you are found eligible, then you are assigned a "Service Coordinator." That individual will meet with you and ask you about your wants, needs, and goals in life. They will then assist you as best they can to help you to achieve them.

My goal had been to live independently. In my case, it took a while before that would be reasonable for me to do because my brain didn't function too good back then. But as the years passed and I got better, then it became a more reasonable goal, and that's when I moved into Davis with the help of my ALTA caseworkers. It was near the end of my time in Davis that Lou was being investigated by the probation department for mishandling my money. That was the exact month that he had me move back in with the family and pulled me out of ALTA. What a coincidence. Granted I needed surgery on my nose at the time (my breathing problem was related to my accident. It hadn't been very severe right after the accident, but got worse as the years went by), but after I had recovered from my nasal surgery, I wanted to live on my own again like I did in Davis. It was some eighteen months before they signed me up with ALTA again, and then I was able to move into the group home. It wasn't too long after I was there that I really wanted to move out on my own again, because I was very unhappy at the group home, as I didn't feel it was a good placement for me. My new ALTA caseworker, Stacy, understood that and told me about the independent living skill services available that I was already familiar with from my time in Davis. But Lou was against the idea of my living on my own again and wanted me to keep living in the group home. He kept coming up with excuses as to why I shouldn't live independently. Again, it was my ALTA caseworker, Stacy Lee who was my biggest advocate and stood up for me and helped me convince Lou that it would be okay for me to try living on my own, and that I would have a good support system to help me.

I would be willing to bet that Lou was afraid that Stacy would get suspicious of why Lou didn't want me to become more independent again if Lou kept resisting the idea. He needed to be able to operate with as little resistance as possible and in as much secret as possible. He couldn't continue to fight Stacy on it without looking completely unreasonable, and then she would wonder why he was fighting it so hard. Which she did. But we never had any proof at the time. Perhaps he also thought that I would be so grateful to be living on my own on the fraction of my money that I would settle in and never ask about my money situation. But, I had set goals for myself, again, with the help of my ALTA caseworker, Stacy, and those were to get a communication device and buy a home after I had been living on my own successfully for a year. Stacy agreed that those were good goals, and she fully supported them with me and tried to talk to my parents about them, but they refused on both accounts. She thought that was more than a bit unreasonable. By this time, Lou had said some things in meetings that had upset Stacy and made her suspicious of Lou's intentions for me. After I received the accounting by mistake and had proof that Lou was taking advantage of my estate, then that became the motivation to get a new conservator and become even more independent and learn about my money for myself. Again, it was ALTA to the rescue as Stacy was extremely supportive of my going through with my court case as well. In hindsight, I believe that Lou didn't want me to become more independent and didn't want me to have help so that I would never find out about what he had been doing with my money. And if that was his fear, then he was right, because my independence certainly did lead to my finding out and ultimately his dismissal as my conservator. And when I accomplished that goal, then I was ready to buy a home, get married, and have a family. In that order.

Thank God that I did have Stacy Lee as my ALTA caseworker during that time, because she was willing to go against my parents on my behalf. And she encouraged me to fight to get a different conservator as well. I also thank God that Bill was my conservator during the time I was married to Danielle. I can't begin to imagine what Lou's response would have been to my wanting to get married and buy a house. My point is that these are the goals that I had set for myself and my service coordinators have always done their best to help me accomplish them, even if that meant going against my parents. And that doesn't always happen. Some service coordinators don't want to rock the boat as far as supporting someone who wants to change their conservatorship. They don't want to upset the families. But it seems to me the rights of the disabled person should come before the preferences of the parents. As long as the desires are reasonable, because I do know some folks who have unreasonable expectations or demands of what they want. In that case, it's more difficult for ALTA to be diplomatic and assist the individual while helping them maintain their desires as best they can. In reading my ALTA files, I have respect and gratitude for the way that my ALTA caseworkers always did their best not just for me, but to support me and to find the truth when they felt my parents were not being exactly honest with them. It seems after a certain point they did not just rubber-stamp what my parents wanted, but genuinely listened to me and what my desires were, and then they did their best to support and help me accomplish them. This has meant a lot to me, especially after watching what happened with Danielle. That could have been me too if it hadn't been for Stacy being so tenacious and not caring what my parents thought.

Service coordinators will also help with some transportation (such as bus passes and dial-a-ride and taxis for some special cases that are work related). Funding for supported workshops, funding for supported employment, and some kinds of counseling. They also pay for some conferences such as People First and the Supported Life conference. They will also help with respite for folks living at home and for disabled kids as well as some summer camps. Respite is a place where adults who live at home with their parents can go to spend the weekend away and do social activities with others. The respite for children is where ALTA will pay for someone to come and stay with a disabled child so that the parents can get a bit of a break from their kids.

The service coordinators will usually meet with you once every three months or talk to you on the phone to see how you are doing. They will come and meet with you wherever you happen to be living if that is what you want.

Some service coordinators are better than others, and I think I've only had one that I had any difficulties with, and that was mostly during the time of the problems with Danielle. She is the one who said that if I was having difficulties, I should have called her. Which is challenging when you can't talk. Most of the time I would get her answering machine, and it is very difficult for me to leave a message that would have made sense to her, or to be able to answer her questions if she had called me back. Romana was out of town on her annual Thanksgiving vacation when everything with Danielle occurred, so she was not there to communicate for me. Bill did call ALTA for me, but his feeling was that considering the crisis that I was having at the time, my caseworker should have called to check on me to see how I was doing.

ALTA is a voluntary organization, meaning you don't have to get ALTA services if you don't want to. Everything is really up to you. On the other hand, I still think that ALTA has an obligation to make sure that if you want to leave ALTA (once you are signed up with them) that it is *your* true choice and not the choice of someone else. As in Danielle's case where her father pulled her out with no documentation that he had the right to do so, only stating verbally that he was her guardian, which we know was not possible because she was in her twenties at the time and not a minor. Nor did Danielle herself ever talk to her caseworker to say she wanted to be dropped from ALTA services.

This seems like a gross mishandling of the situation. A week before Danielle's parents took her away, Danielle and I had a meeting with our ALTA caseworkers, in our home, without her parents present to tell our caseworkers that her parents were interfering way too much in our lives, and that we wanted and needed distance from them. We were asking for ALTA's help in dealing with this. This was clearly understood by the caseworkers at that time. The next week, a meeting was held at ALTA to help us explain to her parents that we wanted and needed time alone to be a married couple. This was not an unreasonable request. We would also have our ILS workers to help us, so it was not like we wanted to be alone with no support or help. We just wanted our instructors instead of her parents. That was the more independent way of doing things, so we all thought. Her parents got very upset about that at first, but then, as I have recounted before, her parents suddenly stopped arguing and agreed. We should have known then that something was up. But they acted like everything was all right. It was that weekend that her mother took her shopping, and then her father called to say she didn't want to come back. This should be noted that again, he did this during Thanksgiving week when not just Romana would be out of town, but would be a short week for ALTA as well, and that since they had been our advocates, that they would not be around to help.

I believe it was when ALTA called the Alexanders to talk with Danielle that Mr. Alexander told them that Danielle didn't want to be involved with ALTA any more either. I was shocked that ALTA took the word of the very person Danielle had told ALTA she did not want having so much control over her life, and essentially turned her over to him without a fight, or at least a private meeting or conversation with her. This was inconsistent with everything Danielle had always said. She did not want to be under her father's control again, and yet that's where she ended up. She always said she wanted to move to New York to get as far away from him as possible. She said her greatest nightmare came true when she woke up from her coma and knew she was now under her father's control for good, unless something happened. Like us getting married. I still don't understand how ALTA could take the word of the very person she most wanted to escape from that she didn't want me or ALTA anymore. We have been told that it became an Adult Protective Services matter. But if ALTA is an advocate for clients, then how can they accept the word of the person she most dreaded to pull her out of ALTA without talking to her privately. Bill put it best when he constantly repeated that undue influence was being used against Danielle. In the same week, she had said both in the privacy of her home and in the meeting at ALTA that she **did not want to be under her father's influence**! And yet, that is exactly what ALTA allowed to happen. As did Area Board 3, who is also supposed to be a watchdog for the rights of the disabled. So . . .

What are the rights of the disabled? Who enforces them? What happens if their rights are being abused? Who makes sure that their rights are being looked after? If someone was an ALTA client and supposedly had these rights, and yet they were controlled and unduly influenced, who is responsible for setting things right? While I am very happy and content in my current life, I cannot help but grieve for the lost life and dreams of Danielle. It is not for me that I write of this, but for her. I can only hope that in some small way, this book might be of assistance to help set her free. I promised her long ago I would do my best, and while I am a happily married man and father, the pleas of Danielle to save her from her parents still haunts both Romana and I. And we still feel we have an obligation to her, although there is not much more we can do then to write about it.

This brings me to APS, Adult Protective Services. I have written about them earlier in the chapter about Danielle. I don't know what the current regulations are at the time, but the person we had investigate the case of Danielle had extreme prejudice and we all felt never gave a proper investigation of the case, nor did we ever find anyone we could appeal that decision to. I can only hope that in the intervening ten years, things have gotten better. Since I wrote so much about it before, I don't see much point to revisiting it again in this chapter. But their job is supposed to be to investigate if anyone is being abused either mentally, emotionally, sexually or financially. Just the suspicion is supposed to be enough to trigger an investigation of a senior or disabled person. I certainly hope that things have gotten better then they were.

Independent Living Skills Training Programs aka ILS:

This is the program through which I have gotten the most assistance. Over the years the support has been very helpful. It is meant to be training and support to help people transition from living dependently either with their families or in group homes to living independently either on their own or with a roommate. This is all decided via the regional centers and your own IPP meeting that is held there. There are a wide variety of goals that one can choose to work on. Once you are living independently, then the support continues to help you live your life successfully. Sometimes things are calm and steady, and other times there may be crises in life to deal with. Your ILS instructor is there to help you under both conditions.

There is what's called Supported Living Services. This provides twenty-four-hour care for folks with more severe disabilities. We have included some other information below about ILS and SLS services. This is strictly informational. We do not recommend or support or endorse any of the agencies listed below; we simply provide them so our readers can see what some of the options available are. Your local regional center will have more useful information about what agencies and individuals are vendored and available to help you with whatever your needs may be in these areas.

Sheltered Workshop:

When I first began attending Mother Lode Rehabilitation Enterprises aka MORE Workshop in Placerville in March of 1983, it was five years after my accident. My parents had only recently moved us to El Dorado County and I was starting to go stir crazy from being home with my parents all the time. I was always a very social person, and being isolated with just my parents had gotten pretty old. So I was glad to be able to go away during the day and meet new people and learn new things.

My first day at the workshop, I was nervous because I couldn't talk, and I was afraid that they would think I was a baby because I couldn't talk. I was concerned about how I would communicate my thoughts and feelings to these new people. But the staff worked hard to make me feel comfortable, and they were patient with learning to understand me. I don't remember much about the other clients there at the time, but I don't remember anything bad about any of them either.

I was glad first and foremost for the opportunity to work and make money. I couldn't have handled a job anywhere else at the time. The workshop was geared for folks like me who were just getting started in the work world. While I had worked at the veterinarian office for about a year before my accident, everything changed for me because of the accident, and I essentially had to start all over again. The workshop was a good place for that. They were very patient with some of my more difficult behaviors. The staff was specially trained to deal with folks with challenging personalities such as I had at the time.

The workshop is geared for folks of all learning levels, from the severely disabled to the mildly disabled. They work with folks with a wide variety of differing abilities. The staff is well trained to handle many sorts of diverse folks. The work is variable depending on skill levels, and they never make someone do more then they can do, but they will try to get you to learn and expand your abilities. They want to help folks learn to be the best they can be. For instance, I stunk at many things when I first started, but as the years went by, I got much better and my abilities increased significantly. At first I wasn't very good at either the book binder or the shredder, but again, I got much better as time went by. I found I even surprised myself in what I learned I could do. And the staff was always encouraging me to learn and do more and be a better person. It is a safe and mostly rewarding experience. We did have differences of opinion of how I thought things should be sometimes, but overall it was extremely beneficial to me. They wouldn't let me get away with my temper tantrums and gave me constructive ways to handle it appropriately. Even when I didn't agree with them, they were right most of the time. They taught me many important things about being in the work world. Like how important it is to present a good working image. They also kept tabs on my medications to make sure I was taking what I was supposed to. Some folks had real hygiene difficulties, and the staff was good at helping them learn what was expected in the work world as far as that goes as well. Most of the staff was always kind with a few temperamental exceptions that are no longer there.

One of the biggest challenges of the workshop is for the individuals there to learn to get along with each other. Just like in real world employment, the supported workshop had a very diverse group of folks who go there. And they don't always get along very well. But again, the staff is trained to deal with difficult personalities. The staff has lots of good tools they use to help people work out their differences in a positive way. And one of the best things about the workshop is that it's a good place for people to go during the day to be productive citizens, which I think we should all do our best to be. I personally think its better than just sitting around watching TV all day. The pay isn't very good, but the experience is well worth it if you are just learning the ropes of life. Like any other job, the harder and faster you work, the more you can earn. By the time I left, I was making significantly more than when I started.

The sheltered workshop experience does teach about getting there on time, punching in and out on timesheets, taking breaks at specific times, and learning to get along with your coworkers. These are all the things that anyone who works needs to learn about. Some of it was familiar to me from working at the veterinarian office, but was set up to help someone with disabilities handle learning new things. The baby steps helped me get used to a routine of working again. And it made me feel valuable too. And they gave me work I could do without getting too frustrated. That's not to say I didn't get frustrated. I could be very stubborn, and sometimes I thought things should be done a certain way, but that was not the way they did things, and one of the things I had to learn was to accept that and not argue with the staff. Which was very difficult for me. Sometimes I'd get really angry and then I had to go outside and calm down.

At the workshop, they also taught some basic classes like simple cooking or "friendship" classes, but I didn't want to take any; I just wanted to work and make money. I was still having difficulties with my temper, and the staff was very patient with me and helped me find ways to cope with my anger as best they could. MORE mostly does recycling of paper goods. They have some of what they call "contract" work which are simple jobs the clients there can do. That may be putting birdseed in small bags to go with bird feeders. The jobs they have change frequently depending on the needs of the community. I never did contract work, however, as I always chose to work out on the production floor. The only difficulty I know of was that there were times it was very hot in summer and very cold in winter as there was no air or heat due to the huge size of the production area.

Now, it is twenty-six years later. And I have come a long way from who I was back then. I left the workshop three months after I started there back in July of 1983 when I moved to Davis, and returned again six years later in April of 1989. I stayed there until around June of 1996 when I left to move into the house in Cameron Park a couple of months before Danielle and I got married. I now have my own wife and child to keep me busy at home.

For many people, the workshop is the only social outlet that they have. Some folks start out at the workshop and move into Supported Employment and don't go to the workshop anymore. Others prefer to just stay there and have no desires to move out into the working world, as they are more comfortable in the supported workshop environment. It is a place where you can do either or both. In my case, in the couple of years before I left to move to Cameron Park, I worked in the community at Super Plumbing in the mornings, and then I would go to the workshop in the afternoons. It kept me busy and among friends and allowed me to make extra money.

Overall, I would strongly recommend the sheltered workshop environment to learn and grow in until you feel you are ready for more.

Supported Employment:

I have mentioned Supported Employment in the past, and now I will share more information about it. It is much like it sounds. It is partially funded by the Department of Rehabilitation.

Supported Employment starts by doing an evaluation of your skills and knowledge and preferences of what sort of work you may want to do, or know how to do. They will give you a realistic view of what you can do and what you can learn to do. They will help you look for a job and sometimes try out different jobs. They will assign you a job coach to help you. A job coach will show you how to do your job and will be there to make sure you learn how to do it right. And they will work with your boss as well so that they understand you and that you are learning to do the job. If things in your job are changed, then the job coach will come and help you learn those new things. Or if procedures are changed, they will help you learn that. If you belong to a union, they will go to union meetings with you and will help you learn and understand about being in a union. Once you know what you are doing, then you don't need your job coach around very much, but if anything changes and you need help again, they will come back to help as much as they can. Therefore, you are "supported" in your employment.

This ends our personal narrative on the different agencies and what we have thought of them. The next part is factual information taken from the Web sites of the different agencies themselves. You will find more agencies than what we have actually commented on. Some of them we have had little or no experience with, but during our online research found them to be of possible use to those reading this book, so we decided to include them.

PART TWO
IN THEIR OWN WORDS
TAKEN FROM THE WEB SITES OF THESE AGENCIES

SOCIAL SECURITY BENEFITS

Here are some excerpts from the SSA Web page (www.ssa.gov) about disability and what they do and don't cover.

What We Mean By Disability

The definition of disability under Social Security is different than other programs. Social Security pays only for total disability. No benefits are payable for partial disability or for short-term disability.

"Disability" under Social Security is based on your inability to work. We consider you disabled under Social Security rules if:

* You cannot do work that you did before;
* We decide that you cannot adjust to other work because of your medical condition(s); and
* Your disability has lasted or is expected to last for at least one year or to result in death.

This is a strict definition of disability. Social Security program rules assume that working families have access to other resources to provide support during periods of short-term disabilities, including workers' compensation, insurance, savings, and investments.

OUR NOTE: There are lots of ways that folks are disabled, but here we are covering information for those with a developmental disability.

Adults Disabled Before Age Twenty-two

An adult disabled before age twenty-two may be eligible for child's benefits if a parent is deceased or starts receiving retirement or disability benefits. We consider this a "child's" benefit because it is paid on a parent's Social Security earnings record.

We make the disability decision using the disability rules for adults.

The "adult child"—including an adopted child, or, in some cases, a stepchild, grandchild, or step-grandchild—must be unmarried, age eighteen or older, and have a disability that started before age twenty-two.

Frequently Asked Questions:

What if the adult child never worked?

It is not necessary that the adult child ever worked because benefits are paid on the parent's earnings record.

What if the adult child is currently working?

The adult child must not have substantial earnings. The amount of earnings we consider "substantial" increases each year. In 2008, this means working and earning more than $940 a month.

Certain expenses the adult child incurs in order to work may be excluded from these earnings. For more information about work and disability, refer to *Working While Disabled—How We Can Help*.

What if the adult child is already receiving SSI benefits?

An adult child already receiving SSI benefits should still check to see if benefits may be payable on a parent's earnings record. Higher benefits might be payable, and entitlement to Medicare may be possible.

What if the adult child is already receiving disability benefits on his or her own record?

An adult child already receiving disability benefits should still check to see if benefits may be payable on a parent's earnings record. It is possible for an individual disabled since childhood to attain insured status on his or her own record and be entitled to higher benefits on a parent's record.

What if the parent never worked?

No benefits would be payable on the record of a parent who never worked.

Can an application be completed online for a disabled adult child's benefits?

At this time, you cannot apply for child's benefits online. If you wish to file for benefits for a child, contact Social Security immediately at 1-800-772-1213 (TTY number 1-800-325-0778) so that you do not lose any potential benefits.

Your disabled adult child cannot apply for benefits online, but he or she can get the process started by completing the online Adult Disability Report before contacting us.

How do we decide if an adult "child" is disabled for SSDI benefits?

If a child is age eighteen or older, we will evaluate his or her disability the same way we would evaluate the disability for any adult. We send the application to the Disability Determination Services in your state that completes the disability decision for us. For detailed information about how we evaluate disability for adults, see Disability Benefits (Publication No. 05-10029).

Benefits For Disabled Children

A child under age eighteen may be disabled, but we don't need to consider the child's disability when deciding if he or she qualifies for benefits as your dependent. The child's benefits normally stop at age eighteen unless he or she is a full-time student in an elementary or high school (benefits can continue until age nineteen) or is disabled.

For a child with a disability to receive benefits on your record after age eighteen, the following rules apply:

*   The disabling impairment must have started before age twenty-two, and;
*   He or she must meet the definition of disability for adults.

Note: An adult may become eligible for a disabled child's benefit from Social Security later in life.

For example, a worker starts collecting Social Security retirement benefits at age sixty-two. He has a thirty-eight-year-old son who has had cerebral palsy since birth. The son will start collecting a disabled "child's" benefit on his father's Social Security record.

Supplemental Security Income (SSI)

Supplemental Security Income (SSI)

This booklet explains what Supplemental Security Income (SSI) is, who can get it, and how to apply. It provides basic information and is not intended to answer all questions. For specific information about your situation, you should talk with a Social Security representative.

The SSI program makes payments to people with low income who are age sixty-five or older or are blind or have a disability.

The Social Security Administration manages the SSI program. Even though Social Security manages the program, SSI is not paid for by Social

Security taxes. SSI is paid for by U.S. Treasury general funds, not the Social Security trust funds.

[Back to top]

What is SSI?

SSI makes monthly payments to people who have low income and few resources and are:

* Age sixty-five or older;
* Blind; or
* Disabled.

If you are applying for SSI, you also should ask for *What You Need To Know When You Get Supplemental Security Income* (SSI) (Publication No. 05-11011).

Disabled or blind children also can receive SSI. You can get more information in *Benefits For Children With Disabilities* (Publication No. 05-10026).

The basic SSI amount is the same nationwide. However, many states add money to the basic benefit. You can call us to find out the amounts for your state.

Rules for getting SSI:

Your income and resources.

Whether you can get SSI depends on your income and resources (the things you own).

Income

Income is money you receive, such as wages, Social Security benefits, and pensions. Income also includes such things as food and shelter. The amount of income you can receive each month and still get SSI depends partly on where you live. You can call us to find out the income limits in your state.

Social Security does not count all of your income when we decide whether you qualify for SSI. For example, we do not count:

* The first $20 a month of most income you receive;
* The first $65 a month you earn from working and half the amount over $65;
* Food stamps;
* Shelter you get from private nonprofit organizations; and
* Most home energy assistance.

If you are married, we also include part of your spouse's income and resources when deciding whether you qualify for SSI. If you are younger than age eighteen, we include part of your parents' income and resources. And, if you are a sponsored noncitizen, we may include your sponsor's income and resources.

If you are a student, some of the wages or scholarships you receive may not count.

If you are disabled but work, Social Security does not count wages you use to pay for items or services that help you to work. For example, if you need a wheelchair, the wages you use to pay for the wheelchair do not count as income when we decide whether you qualify for SSI.

Also, Social Security does not count any wages a blind person uses for work expenses. For example, if a blind person uses wages to pay for transportation to and from work, the wages used to pay the transportation cost are not counted as income.

If you are disabled or blind, some of the income you use (or save) for training or to buy things you need to work may not count.

Resources (things you own)

Resources that we count in deciding whether you qualify for SSI include real estate, bank accounts, cash, stocks, and bonds.

You may be able to get SSI if your resources are worth no more than $2,000. A couple may be able to get SSI if they have resources worth no more than $3,000. If you own property that you are trying to sell, you may be able to get SSI while trying to sell it.

Social Security does not count everything you own in deciding whether you have too many resources to qualify for SSI. For example, we do not count:

*   The home you live in and the land it is on;
*   Life insurance policies with a face value of $1,500 or less;
*   Your car (usually);
*   Burial plots for you and members of your immediate family; and
*   Up to $1,500 in burial funds for you and up to $1,500 in burial funds for your spouse.

Other rules you must meet:

To get SSI, you must live in the U.S. or the Northern Mariana Islands and be a U.S. citizen or national. In some cases, noncitizen residents can qualify for SSI. For more information, ask for Supplemental Security Income (SSI) For Noncitizens (Publication No. 05-11051).

If you are eligible for Social Security or other benefits, you should apply for them. You can get SSI and other benefits if you are eligible for both.

If you live in certain types of institutions, you may get SSI.

If you live in a city or county rest home, halfway house, or other public institution, you usually cannot get SSI. But there are some exceptions.

If you live in a publicly operated community residence that serves no more than sixteen people, you may get SSI.

If you live in a public institution mainly to attend approved educational or job training to help you get a job, you may get SSI.

If you live in a public emergency shelter for the homeless, you may get SSI.

If you live in a public or private institution and Medicaid is paying more than half the cost of your care, you may get a small SSI benefit.

How to apply for SSI:

If you are applying for SSI, you can complete a large part of your application by visiting our website at www.socialsecurity.gov. You also can call us toll-free at 1-800-772-1213 to ask for an appointment with a Social Security representative.

Parents or guardians usually can apply for blind or disabled children under age eighteen. In some cases, other third parties can apply for children.

You should bring certain items when you apply. Even if you do not have all of the things listed below, apply anyway. The people in the Social Security office can help you get whatever is needed.

Please bring:

* Your Social Security card or a record of your Social Security number;
* Your birth certificate or other proof of your age;
* Information about the home where you live, such as your mortgage or your lease and landlord's name;
* Payroll slips, bank books, insurance policies, burial fund records, and other information about your income and the things you own;
* The names, addresses, and telephone numbers of doctors, hospitals, and clinics that you have been to, if you are applying for SSI because you are disabled or blind;
* Proof of U.S. citizenship or eligible noncitizen status.

You also should bring your checkbook or other papers that show your bank, credit union, or savings and loan account number so we can have your benefits deposited directly into your account. Direct deposit protects benefits from loss, theft, and mail delay. The money is always on time and ready to use without making a trip to the bank.

A note for people who are blind or disabled:

If you work, there are special rules to help you. You may be able to keep getting SSI payments while you work. As you earn more money, your SSI payments may be reduced or stopped, but you may be able to keep your Medicaid coverage.

You also may be able to set aside some money for a work goal or to go to school. In this case, the money you set aside will not reduce the amount of your SSI.

Blind or disabled people who apply for SSI may get free special services to help them work. These services may include counseling, job training, and help in finding work.

You can get more information in *Working While Disabled—How We Can Help* (Publication No. 05-10095).

Right to appeal:

If you disagree with a decision made on your claim, you can appeal it. The steps you can take are explained in *Your Right To Question A Decision Made On Your Supplemental Security Income (SSI) Claim* (Publication No. 05-11008).

You have the right to be represented by an attorney or other qualified person of your choice. More information is in *Your Right To Representation* (Publication No. 05-10075).

[Back to top]

You may be able to get other help:

If you get SSI, you also may be able to get help from your state or county. For example, you may be able to get Medicaid, food stamps, or other social services. Call your local social services department or public welfare office for information about the services available in your community.

Food stamps:

If everyone in your home signs up for SSI or gets SSI, Social Security will help you fill out the food stamp application.

If you do not live in a home where everyone signs up for SSI or gets SSI, you must go to your local food stamp office to get food stamps. You can get more information about food stamps by visiting our website or calling us to get *Food Stamps and Other Nutrition Programs* (Publication No. 05-10100).

Medicaid:

When you get SSI, you also may get Medicaid, which helps pay doctor and hospital bills. Your local welfare or medical assistance office can give you information about Medicaid.

Help paying for Medicare:

If you get Medicare and have low income and few resources, your state may pay your Medicare premiums and, in some cases, other Medicare expenses such as deductibles and coinsurance. Only your state can decide if you qualify. To find out if you do, contact your state or local welfare office or Medicaid agency. You can get more information about these programs from the Centers for Medicare & Medicaid Services (CMS) by calling the Medicare toll-free number, 1-800-MEDICARE (1-800-633-4227). If you are deaf or hard of hearing, you may call TTY 1-877-486-2048.

You also may be able to get extra help paying for the annual deductibles, monthly premiums, and prescription co-payments related to the Medicare prescription drug program (Part D). You may qualify for extra help if you have limited income (tied to the federal poverty level) and limited resources. These income and resource limits change each year and are not the same as the SSI income and resource limits. You can contact Social Security for the current numbers.

If you have both Medicaid with prescription drug coverage and Medicare, Medicare and SSI, or if your state pays for your Medicare premiums, you automatically will get this extra help and you don't need to apply.

You may be able to get Social Security:

If you have worked and paid into Social Security long enough, you also may be eligible for Social Security benefits while you are receiving SSI. Retirement benefits can be paid to people age sixty-two or older and their families. Disability benefits go to people with disabilities and their families. Survivor's benefits are paid to the families of workers who have died. If you think you may qualify for Social Security benefits, call us to make an appointment to talk with a Social Security representative.

APS (ADULT PROTECTIVE SERVICES)
For the State of California

Each county has an APS agency to help elder adults (sixty-five years and older) and dependent adults (eighteen to sixty-four who are disabled), when these elders and dependent adults are unable to meet their own needs, or are victims of abuse, neglect, or exploitation.

County APS agencies investigate reports of abuse of elders and dependent adults who live in private homes and hotels or hospitals and health clinics when the abuser is not a staff member. (The Licensing & Certification program of the California Department of Health Services handles cases of abuse by a member of a hospital or health clinic.) County APS staff evaluates abuse cases and arranges for services such as advocacy, counseling, money management, out-of-home placement, or conservatorship.

Reports of abuse that occur in a nursing home, a board and care home, a residential facility for the elderly, or at a long-term care facility are the responsibility of the Ombudsman's office, which is administered by the California Department of Aging.

APS staff also provides information and referral to other agencies and educates the public about reporting requirements and responsibilities under the Elder and Dependent Adult Abuse Reporting laws.

These services are available to any elder or dependent adult regardless of income.

Where To Get Help:

If you want to make a report about elder abuse, contact the office listed for your county. Abuse reports may also be made to the local law enforcement agency.

HIGHLIGHTS

*   Services are available to any person, regardless of income.
*   Services are available in all fifty-eight counties.
*   Approximately ninety thousand reports of abuse were received statewide during state fiscal year 2002-2003.

Services for the Developmentally Disabled in the state of California are run under the Department of Developmental Services. That is where ALTA Regional Center comes in.

DDS
(DEPARTMENT OF DEVELOPMENTAL SERVICES)

The California Department of Developmental Services is the agency through which the state of California provides services and supports to individuals with developmental disabilities.

These disabilities include mental retardation, cerebral palsy, epilepsy, autism, and related conditions. Services are provided through state-operated developmental centers and community facilities, and contracts with twenty-one nonprofit regional centers. The regional centers serve as a local resource to help find and access the services and supports available to individuals with developmental disabilities and their families.

ALTA CALIFORNIA REGIONAL CENTERS

Working for a future where all individuals are valued members of their communities.

ALTA is one of a network of twenty-one regional centers in California established by the Lanterman Mental Retardation Services Act of 1969. ALTA is a private nonprofit corporation working under contract with the California Department of Developmental Services.

ALTA California Regional Center creates and maintains partnerships to support all persons with developmental disabilities, children at risk, and their families in choosing services and supports through individual lifelong planning to achieve satisfying lifestyles in their own communities.

ALTA provides services to over sixteen thousand persons with developmental disabilities and their families throughout a ten county area (click here to view the 10 counties served). Each county is unique. ACRC works to develop local services and supports that help meet our mission.

Over the past several years our regional center has experienced tremendous growth. With this growth the dissemination of information becomes more vital.

ILS/SLS Services

Please note that we do not endorse the agencies below; we simply have them here to provide information about ILS/SLS.

The STEP Independent Living Services (ILS) program provides instruction for individuals with developmental disabilities, and specializes in working with deaf and deaf/blind who choose to live on their own in the community. This includes one-to-one instruction in various settings based on the personal needs of the individual.

These services generally begin with a formal assessment of skills which have been determined necessary for an individual to live on his or her own within the community. This assessment can be started while an individual lives in a care home or family home, but will not be completed until the individual has moved into his or her own home. This assessment and our services include such areas as domestic skills, personal skills, health and safety, financial skills, community skills and awareness, and responsibility areas. In addition, there are portions of this assessment for individuals who use wheelchairs as well as those with specialized communication needs. Any individual who is deaf or deaf/blind would be assessed by someone who is fluent in ASL.

Following the completion of the assessment, STEP will work with the client toward developing an Individual Service Plan (ISP) which outlines the skills that our instructor and the client will be working toward for the next six months. This plan and the goals in it are based on the needs of that individual, and the skills necessary for that individual to successfully live on his or her own within the community.

ALTA California Regional Center has determined that thirty-five hours of ILS services per month is the maximum that an individual can receive, but that agency has made exceptions to this rule.

The ongoing responsibilities of the ILS instructor include assisting each individual with meeting the goals on the service plan to the best of that person's ability, and ensuring that each client is aware of community services which are available to him or her. The instructor can also be helpful in assisting in an individual's transition from a more sheltered environment into the community. This process may involve assisting with finding a suitable home in the community, and helping to ensure that each person is acclimated to his or her new surroundings.

http://www.stepagency.com/ils.htm

AREA BOARDS

This brings us to the Area Boards—what are they and what do they do? Well, that appears to be a good question. Romana and I have been doing internet research to try and answer this question, and although we have found the Web page for Area Board 3 (in whose jurisdiction I live), there's nothing on the page as far as a "Mission Statement" that tells us exactly what it is that they do. What we did find however, was this:

What is the State Council on Developmental Disabilities?

The State Council on Developmental Disabilities (SCDD) is established by state and federal law as an independent state agency to ensure that people with developmental disabilities and their families receive the services and supports they need.

Consumers know best what supports and services they need to live independently and to actively participate in their communities. Through advocacy, capacity building, and systemic change, SCDD works to achieve a consumer and family-based system of individualized services, supports, and other assistance.

My laymen's experience is that they are a "watchdog" for the regional centers. It appears that each state has his or her own federally funded State Council, so everyone can go look up his or her local one.

While doing research on Protection and Advocacy we came across this interesting bit of history that we were previously unaware of, but deem it important enough to include here so that others with disabilities will have knowledge of it and it may be of help to them. I wish I had known about them back when things were so messed up in my life:

PROTECTION AND ADVOCACY INC

History, role, and funding

In 1975, after television news exposed horrific abuse and neglect at Willow Brook, a state institution for people with mental retardation on Staten Island, New York, Senator Jacob Javits successfully pushed Congress to mandate and fund Protection and Advocacy systems in each state.

The laws which give Protection and Advocacy systems the special responsibility to protect and advocate for people with disabilities also give those organizations a unique tool with which to accomplish that task: access to facilities or programs providing care and treatment to persons with disabilities, and access to the confidential records of people with disabilities. This access permits Protection and Advocacy systems to conduct abuse or neglect investigations, provide information and training about the rights of individuals with disabilities, and monitor a facility or program's compliance with respect to the rights and safety of people who receive their services. Protection and Advocacy systems are also unique because courts have recognized that the broad congressional authority allows them to bring actions in their own name to vindicate the rights of people with disabilities.

In May, 1978 California's Protection & Advocacy, Inc. (PAI) became a nonprofit agency with responsibility for providing the advocacy services required under the Developmental Disabilities Assistance and Bill of Rights Act of 1975. PAI was governed by a seven-member board of directors appointed by the governor and received advice and assistance from a review committee.

Here is their mission statement and principals:
PAI's Mission Statement
"Advancing the human and legal rights of people with disabilities."
PAI's Vision Statement
"PAI will:

CHANGE
The system so it values diversity, culture, and each individual.
CREATE
A barrier free, inclusive world where people with disabilities enjoy

* Equality,
* Dignity,
* Power,
* Freedom of choice,
* Independence, and
* Freedom from abuse, neglect, and discrimination.

Quality, culturally responsive, safe, affordable, accessible

* Housing,
* Benefits,
* Education,
* Health care,
* Transportation, and
* Individual and family supports, chosen and directed by the person with a disability.

Opportunities for satisfying

* Work,
* Community service, and
* Family and social relationships.

ADVANCE
The human and legal rights of people with disabilities."
This seems like a good organization. They also offer legal advice and some services for low-income individuals.

PEOPLE FIRST

What is People First ®?

People First is a self-advocacy and self-help organization of people who have developmental disabilities. "Self-advocacy" means that the members are learning how to speak for themselves and make decisions about what they want to do with their lives. "Self-help" means that the members are helping each other with their problems, making friends and reaching out to people with severe disabilities. The members also plan fund-raisers and social events like dances or picnics or other activities.

How did People First get started?

The People First organization was born in 1974 when a group of people, many of whom lived in an institution in Oregon, went to a conference about "self-advocacy" in Canada. When they got back and talked about the conference, they were upset because professionals had run all the sessions. They thought that people with disabilities should have run them. They decided to organize their own conference and run it themselves.

One of the first things they needed to do was come up with a name. At a large meeting, at the Oregon institution, people with developmental disabilities got together to pick a name. After several suggestions, Judy Cunio, a woman with a developmental disability, spoke up and said,

"We are people first, our disabilities are second. Why can't they just call us People First." As the name People First was whispered from person to person, everybody liked it and chose it as the name for their self-advocacy group. There are now People First chapters across the United States and around the world.

THE PUBLIC GUARDIAN-CONSERVATOR-ADMINISTRATOR

(from the County Offices: Public Guardian-Conservator-Administrator web page)

County Offices: Public Guardian-Conservator-Administrator

The Public Guardian-Conservator-Administrator provides mandated conservatorship and estate administration services as specified by the Probate Code and Welfare and Institution's Code. The organization of these services varies among counties. The Public Guardian, Public Conservator, and/or Public Administrator is personally responsible for these functions, which are delegated within the department.

The services of the Public Guardian may be provided through a separate county department, an elected official, or incorporated into a larger department such as health or human services. Public Conservator services are oftentimes provided by the Public Guardian, but the responsibilities may be shared with mental health departments. The Public Administrator may be an elected official, a separate department, or housed within another county department such as sheriff-coroner, treasurer, or public guardian-conservator.

Office Responsibilities

The Public Guardian-Conservator serves as conservator of a person and/or estate of individuals needing protective intervention. The two types of conservatorship, Lanterman-Petris-Short (LPS) and probate, can only be established by order of the superior court. As probate conservator, Public Guardians are involved in all aspects of their clients' lives, including financial management, housing, medical care, placement, and advocacy. As LPS conservator, Public Conservators are responsible for directing the mental health treatment and placement of their clients. Referrals for probate conservatorship usually come from another community agency, institution, or physician. Referrals for LPS conservatorship can only come from a psychiatrist who is affiliated with a Short-Doyle hospital.

The Public Administrator is responsible for administering the estate of a county resident who dies without a will or family in California. Estate administration may include marshaling all assets, selling real or personal property, performing heir searches, and overseeing the distribution of the estate. The activities are supervised by the superior court. The Public Administrator may also supervise the county's indigent burial program.

IHSS (IN-HOME SUPPORT SERVICES)

Provides assistance to eligible adults sixty-five years or older, or blind or disabled individuals, who are unable to remain safely in their homes without assistance.

In-Home Supportive Services (IHSS) serves aged, blind, or disabled persons who are unable to perform activities of daily living and cannot remain safely in their own homes without help. Through IHSS, qualified recipients may receive assistance with daily tasks, such as:

* bathing
* dressing
* cooking
* cleaning
* grooming
* feeding

To be eligible for IHSS services, a person must receive SSI or meet income and resource guidelines. In addition, the individual must be either:

* sixty-five years or older
* blind
* permanently disabled, or
* a disabled child requiring extraordinary care

Anyone who recognizes that a person is in need of in-home assistance may refer a client to IHSS. Once a referral is received, a social worker assigned to the case conducts an assessment to determine the applicant's need. The determination will take into consideration the applicant's medical condition, living arrangement, and resources that may already be available.

Once eligibility has been established, IHSS can assist a client with locating a caregiver. A friend or relative may serve as a caregiver, or a referral may be selected through the IHSS registry. Once a caregiver is selected, the client acts as the employer and is responsible for supervision and signing time sheets. IHSS will arrange for payment.

Working together, IHSS and the caregiver ensure that each client is able to remain in familiar surroundings—safely, comfortably, and with as much independence as possible.

MORE WORKSHOP

Our Vision: Full Inclusion for People with Disabilities
Our Mission: Empowering Individuals with Disabilities to Enhance Their Quality of Life

MORE is a private, nonprofit organization dedicated to supporting persons with disabilities. MORE was established by a group of parents, educators, rehabilitation professionals, and concerned citizens and first began serving adults with disabilities in 1973. The organization has grown from serving less than ten to now over two hundred individuals on a daily basis. Our services include direct training in social, living, and vocational skills. In addition, we assist the community in providing real life opportunities, including work, for those we serve.

MORE is governed by a volunteer board of directors. Its membership includes concerned citizens, caregivers, and persons served. It is the purpose of the board of directors to create governing policies that assure the continuation and the continual improvement of quality services to those we serve. Board meetings are held the third Monday every other month beginning at 5:00 p.m. at our main facility at 399 Placerville Drive, in Placerville.

General membership in our organization is available to the public and any individual interested in furthering the purpose of MORE. Annually, the membership elects new directors and votes on all bylaw revisions.

MORE publishes an annual report which contains a description of our program services, a financial report, and much other useful information. If you are interested in receiving a copy of this report, please call us at 622-4848.

Thank you for visiting. Please come again!

Community Access Program

CAP is our Adult Development Center, providing a 1:4 staff-to-client ratio. Activities include basic living skills, social activities, vocational training, banking, survival reading, food service, and other basic skills. The focus is on integration into the community, and much time is spent on outings to museums, cultural festivals, the theater, shopping, banking, volunteering, and other community-based activities.

Creative Arts

Students receive instruction in singing, music, painting, photography, drama, and much more. Their work is displayed in The Something MORE Art Gallery and they perform in several presentations throughout the year.

The people we serve are being transformed, as they discover their hidden talents and skills. They are students of creative arts classes on their way to becoming artists, musicians, painters or, sculptors.

Work Activity Program

As its name implies, the focus here is on work and vocational training. We provide training in sorting, collating, assembly, packaging, grounds keeping, contract work, and document destruction.

Prevocational Program

Our Prevocational Program works hand in hand with our Work Activity Program to provide training in social skills, job readiness, food service, DMV testing, public transportation training, and many other valuable skills. Clients have a chance to go out in the community to do their banking, shopping, and plan luncheon engagements with their peers.

Personal Vocational Social Adjustment Services

This is a very specialized, time-limited program which addresses any barriers a person might have to community employment. Students receive one-on-one instruction and counseling to help them assimilate into the community.

Supported Employment Program

This program provides a job coach to accompany the person to the job site and train them to do their job efficiently at no cost to the employer. Employers hiring our clients receive government credits for doing so. As job skills are learned and proficiency increases, the job coach begins to fade away, leaving the client to do his job independently.

Pathways Residential Home

Pathways is home to twelve adults with disabilities on their way to independent living in the community. Clients learn how to cook and keep their apartment clean, how to shop, important social skills, grooming and hygiene, and many other valuable independent living skills. Curriculum includes outings in the community as well as shopping and banking independently, use of public transit, and taking care of medical and business appointments.

CALIFORNIA DEPARTMENT OF REHABILITATION

What Does DOR Do?

The Department of Rehabilitation (DOR) assists Californians with disabilities obtain and retain employment and maximize their ability to live independently in their communities. Working with individuals of every type and category of disability, DOR provides vocational rehabilitation services to eligible Californians. DOR also provides ADA technical assistance and training and funds twenty-nine independent living centers, which offer information and referral services to assist individuals with disabilities live active, independent lives.

Vocational rehabilitation services are designed to get Californians with disabilities prepared for employment and can include training, education, transportation, and job placement.

DOR had provided services to adults with developmental disabilities as part of the Habilitation Program through June 30, 2004. Information on this program, now administered by Department of Developmental Services (DDS), is available on the DDS Habilitation Services website at http://www.dds.ca.gov/Habilitation/HabSvs_Home.cfm.

If you are from out of state, have transportation questions, are in the correctional system or have a specific concern, please go to our Frequently Asked Questions.

The following is a list of specific programs for our consumers.

- Vocational Rehabilitation
- Blind Services
- Business Enterprises Program (BEP)
- Deaf and Hard of Hearing Services
- Assistive Technology
- Transportation
- Independent Living

DOR FREQUENTLY ASKED QUESTIONS:

Q: What kind of rehabilitation do you do?

A: DOR provides Vocational Rehabilitation Services to Californians with disabilities who want to work. Our services include employment counseling, training, and education, mobility and transportation aids, job search, and placement assistance.

Q: What kind of disabilities do you help with?

A: We serve people with all types and categories of disability.

Q: What age do you need to be? Do you have programs for children?

A: Typically, we serve people of working age. We do not have programs for young children; however, we do have programs in some high schools that help seniors transition from school to work or college.

Q: Do you serve Workers Compensation Clients?

A: If you become disabled as a result of your job, you will receive services through California's Workers Compensation system, which is separate from our department. The Department of Industrial Relations can assist you with workers compensation information.

Q: Do I have to live in California to be eligible?

A: Yes.

Q: Do I have to be a California resident to be eligible?

A: Residency is not a requirement for eligibility for DOR services; however, many of the kinds of programs and services we use, such as classes at state universities, do have residency requirements. For ease of access to programs and services, we suggest consumers to become residents.

Q: Do I have to be a U.S. citizen to be eligible?

A: You do not need to be a citizen; however, you do need to have a valid work permit.

Q: I live in another state and am receiving vocational rehabilitation services. Can I transfer my case to California? Do you cover any moving costs? Can I open a case in California before I move?

A: We do not accept transfers of cases from other states. You need to be living in California before we can open your case; however, if you did have a case opened and active in another state, it may make the process smoother. We may be able to help you continue on toward your original employment goal; however, you will need to go through the standard application and assessment process and will be subject to any waiting list criteria we may have. It's a good idea to have copies of your medical records and any pertinent documentation from your out-of-state case to help with your assessment. We cannot cover any moving costs.

Q: I am an inmate scheduled for parole in the near future. Can I apply for services before I am released? Don't you supply tools for jobs as part of a program for recent parolees?

A: You will need to wait until you have been paroled before you can apply for services. Part of the application requires that you be available for the assessment process. As with any DOR case, you will need to have a documented disability and the disability is an impediment to your employment and our services would benefit you in your search for employment. DOR no longer provides tools as a specific service for a parolee; however, if you are found eligible and you are in a disability category we are serving, you may receive rehabilitation services as part of an overall employment plan described in the Consumer Information Handbook (in Rich Text Format). Some of those services may include the purchase of tools.

Q: What is this about a waiting list?

A: For more information, go to the DOR Order of Selection Statement.

Q: How do I get services?

A: You need to become a consumer of DOR in order to receive services. Also, the services we provide are part of a detailed rehabilitation plan developed by the consumer and counselor based on the client's specific needs and employment goals.

Q: How do I apply?

A: For information on how to apply, go to the How to Apply for Services Statement.

Q: How long will it take to get a job?

A: Each case is very individualized, based on a consumer's needs and goals. Also, there is a waiting list for services. Based on medical information and other assessments, applicants fall into one of three categories, most severely disabled, severely disabled and disabled. Currently, DOR is able to serve the first two categories. If you are assessed as being in a category we are serving, you may have little or no wait before receiving rehabilitation services. If you are in a category we are not serving, it could be several months. You will periodically receive notification from DOR with an update on the categories we are serving and the status of the waiting list.

After you are a consumer, it can take a few weeks to several months or years depending on the number and level of services you need to get job ready and find employment.

Q: I need information about my rights under the Americans with Disabilities Act.

A: DOR has a Disability Access unit that provides basic information on the ADA. Its primary purpose is to give information and training to State Government agencies. It is not an enforcement entity. The U.S. Department of Justice has an excellent web site that details rights, remedies, and enforcement of the ADA.

Q: Do you provide housing? Medical Services? Vans?

A: DOR only provides vocational rehabilitation services. We do not provide any housing services.

If you are a consumer, and within your plan for employment it is determined that you need some special medical service or transportation to access or participate in vocational rehabilitation services, then we may provide it.

We do not have a van program for individuals. All transportation needs are met as part of an overall consumer case plan. Vans are the most expensive transportation option for consumers. If there is another, equally reasonable, and less-expensive method, such as public transportation or special transit, that is the method we use.

HUD

HUD's web page is *www.hud.gov*

HUD is a federally funded program that helps with a wide variety of programs and grants mostly in regards to housing for low income and the disabled.

HUD's Mission:

HUD's mission is to increase homeownership, support community development, and increase access to affordable housing free from discrimination. To fulfill this mission, HUD will embrace high standards of ethics, management, and accountability and forge new partnerships—particularly with faith-based and community organizations—that leverage resources and improve HUD's ability to be effective on the community level.

Here is a list of some of the programs available on the HUD Web site.

- Programs of HUD publication—Major Grant, Assistance, and Regulatory Programs
- Community planning and development
- Demonstrations and university and programs
- Fair housing
- Government Sponsored Enterprises
- Healthcare facility loans
- Indian Programs
- Lead hazard control
- Multifamily housing
- Public housing
- Securities
- Single family housing programs

Here is an example of a local HUD program, taken from the El Dorado County Housing Authority on February 12, 2008. We provide this as statistical information to give folks some idea of what the program is like out there.

HOUSING CHOICE VOUCHER PROGRAM

Nowka Announces Opening of Housing Choice Voucher Program (Section 8) Waiting List—First Time in Six Years.

El Dorado County Executive Director Doug Nowka announced today, for the first time in six years, the El Dorado County Housing Authority will be accepting Wait List applications for the Housing Choice Voucher Program (formerly known as Section 8) from February 11 through February 25, 2008. On Monday, February 11, applications will *only* be available and accepted at the El Dorado County Fairgrounds in Placerville (directions) and at the South Lake Tahoe Senior Center (directions) from 9:00 a.m. to 4:00 p.m.

"Opening the waiting list is good news for families who may be seeking affordable housing in El Dorado County," according to Joyce Aldrich, program manager. "In addition to our efforts to maintain our stock of affordable housing through low-interest rehabilitation loans, provide low-interest loans to eligible first-time homebuyers, and provide incentives for additional affordable housing stock, the Housing Choice Voucher program is a critical tool in making sure families can afford to live, work, and raise children here."

The Housing Choice Voucher program provides rental assistance to low-income individuals and families who select their own rentals from homes, mobile homes, and apartments on the private market in El Dorado County. The family pays approximately 30 percent of their income in rent to the landlord, and the Housing Authority pays the rest, up to a certain limit, directly to the landlord. Eligibility is determined by family size and income. Applicants will be selected without reference to race, color, religion, national origin, sex, marital status, disability, or handicap.

Beginning Tuesday, February 12, applications will be available at the El Dorado County Housing Authority offices at 550 Main Street, Suite C in Placerville and at 3368 Lake Tahoe Blvd., Suite 202 in South Lake Tahoe. This year, for the first time, they will also be available February 12 through February 25, 2008 by Internet (www.co.el-dorado.ca.us/humanservices/pdf/HCVpreApplication Engllish.pdf). All applications must be received or postmarked by 5:00 p.m. February 25, 2008 to be considered.

No applications will be handed out at the Housing Authority offices in Placerville or South Lake Tahoe on February 11. You must go to the fairgrounds to receive and submit an application in Placerville or to the senior center in South Lake Tahoe to receive and submit an application on that date.

To receive an application by mail, call the El Dorado County Housing Authority between the hours of 8 a.m. and 4:30 p.m. at (530) 642-7150. No applications will be mailed before February 12. If you return your application by mail, it must be postmarked between February 11 and February 25 to be accepted.

Once on the waiting list, it is not unusual for a family to remain on the waiting list for several years. When a family's name reaches the top of the waiting list, applicants' information is verified to determine eligibility. The waiting list was last opened in 2002 when over one thousand names were added.

The El Dorado County Housing Authority office has a fixed number of vouchers available from the U.S. Department of Housing & Urban Development (HUD) and can reissue them only when a family moves off the program or HUD provides additional vouchers to the Housing Authority.

Any family, single, elderly, and/or disabled person, at least eighteen years of age, who is a United States citizen or an eligible immigrant, who meet the income eligibility may apply. To be eligible for assistance, total household annual gross income must be less than or equal to the following HUD income guidelines for El Dorado County: One person, $23,500; Two persons $26,900; Three persons, $30,250; Four persons, $33,600; Five persons, $36,300; Six persons, $39,000; Seven persons, $41,650; and Eight persons, $44,350.

Only one application form will be accepted per applicant. Duplicate applications will be rejected. Families or individuals are placed on the waiting list according to the El Dorado County Housing Authority Local Preference System and by date and time completed applications are received.

The Local Preference System gives preference to the disabled, veterans, victims of domestic violence, applicants who have or will be involuntarily displaced, and applicants with at least one adult who is employed at least twenty-five hours per week, or who are active participants in an accredited educational or training program designed to prepare the individual for the job market. This preference is extended to elderly families or families whose head or spouse is receiving an income based on their inability to work.

For further information or assistance, please contact the El Dorado County Housing Authority at (530) 642-7150 Monday through Friday 8:00 am to 4:30 pm.

Equal Housing Opportunity

Chapter 20

An Overview
(Reflections on my past,
my spiritual journey, and my future)

Looking back through my book, my thoughts are "thank you" to everyone in my life for the parts that they played. And that would include the difficult people as well. The challenges that they placed before me only served to make me stronger and more determined to succeed with my life and goals.

Writing this book has brought up many emotions. Sadness, happiness, anger, frustration, joy, and fulfillment. In the beginning, I stated that one of the reasons for writing this book was as a form of therapy. It certainly has been so. There have been pluses and minuses. Having to write about how I was controlled, mislead, and manipulated were the negative parts. The way that I was disregarded by my stepfather in his handling of my money and living situation. How I was betrayed by Danielle's father who took Danielle away when I would not agree to transfer my conservatorship to him.

I also want to clarify Romana's part in this in regards to my family. My mother especially blamed Romana for keeping me from the family. I want her to know that it was Romana who tried over and over again to get me to interact with my mother. But I was so understandably angry at how my family was treating me that I would get upset with Romana when she would do this. I would tell her to stop. I didn't want her to encourage me to communicate with them or see them. On one level, I understood what she was trying to do, but on the other level, I knew the timing was not right for it yet. I needed my anger at them to help me get through the conservatorship battle. Only when I had won my freedom would I be willing to consider it. Once she finally understood my point and how I needed the anger, she finally agreed and stopped, but she was never happy about it, or the separation from my family.

But I want my mother and others to know that Romana always encouraged me to have a relationship with my mother; she never tried to keep me from her. It was always my own choice. In blaming Romana, they are disregarding my thoughts, feelings, and wishes about the situation. They were making me less than the person that I am and was! And I want other families to think about this, seriously. When you blame the social workers for "keeping" your family member from seeing you, look at your own actions first and see what you may have done to hurt that person's heart so much that *they* don't want to see you. I couldn't understand how my mother could let Lou do this to me, and Romana would try to explain some of the ways this might have happened. I understood but did not agree with her on this, and she would always abide by my decisions, even when she did not agree with it.

Rereading some of the letters my family has written me over the years while researching this book has made me feel very angry and sad. I still don't have a "normal" relationship with my family. I don't feel that I will either until Lou passes away. Lou never attempted to compromise with me in any way in regards to my estate and the handling of my money. If he had offered to come teach me about my money so I could have understood the situation better, then everything might have been different. If he had come and talked to my support team and me about the communication device and the home I wanted to buy, that might have changed things for all of us. He made me feel like an idiot that couldn't learn about these things rather than taking the time to see if I could.

After I had moved out on my own and I had Romana call them many times to invite them to see the apartment I was so proud of, I was hurt and dismayed that they refused to come see it. They used the rational that I might want to move home with them. If they had come to my place and visited me there, they would have seen how well I was doing, and that might have changed their minds also. But in the end, I felt dismissed out of hand by them, and since they were responsible for my money and my rights, I found that very frustrating. If they would not come see how well I was doing, how could I prove to them that I could handle the house I wanted to buy? In fact, as my conservator (not to mention my parent), wasn't it Lou's duty to come see that I was living someplace clean and healthy? Wasn't it my mother's? If the social workers were so horrid, how could my parents trust that I was safe without seeing for themselves? These were some of the thoughts that would go through my head when they didn't' come to visit me. So many things might have been different if they had worked with my support team when I was finally being successful, instead of blaming the team for keeping me from them.

The only time my parents came to see me at my apartment was when they came to try and talk me out of pursing the conservatorship change. And I find that sad. My greatest wish for my book is that this will help others to learn from my family's mistakes so they will not have the rift that mine has.

Looking back at all that I have been through has been a plus in a way. It has given me the opportunity to be grateful for all that I now have, and all that I have accomplished. I have also had a chance to reflect on the support team that surrounded me for many years. Suzie, Vince, Sally, Romana, Bruce, Bill . . . and a variety of job coaches and other folks. All these people helped me in my darkest moments. And when my own family neither visited me, nor seemed to believe in me, they did. And I want to say thank you, yet again, to them for it. I also know that there were people who helped me after my accident that I don't remember. I hope that they remember me, and this is my thanks to them. I hope that when they read this, they will know that the help they gave me then helped me to get to where I am now. Even though I don't remember them, I am very grateful to them, and I would be very happy to hear from them some time so I could offer my thanks to them directly.

One of the lessons that I've had to learn along the way has proved to be an important one. It's one I resisted originally. Romana called it learning to "kiss ass." She first taught it to me when I was at the group home. I wanted to move out, and they wanted me to behave a certain way to do so. I didn't want to. But one day, Romana explained to me the theory of learning to do this. She said if I wanted to get out of the group home, I would have to do whatever they wanted, whether I liked it or not. To grin and bear it. To show I could cooperate, even when I didn't want to. We devised a special sign to represent this, and whenever I was being overly hardheaded about something, Romana would flash that sign to me and I would know this meant to just smile and agree with whatever they were saying at the moment. And amazingly enough, it worked. I have since found it works in many other situations. It worked well during my court hearings for the conservatorship change. As hard as a lesson as this can be to learn, it is a good one.

I have learned to be persistent, to not give up no matter what anyone else thinks. I remember many times people telling me that I wouldn't be able to do something that I had set my mind to. For instance, Lou telling me that I couldn't own a home because I didn't know what it meant to own one. But that didn't stop me from wanting one, or pursing ownership of one. I now own two of them, and a property later sold at a profit. If I listened to him, I'd have none.

The reason I was so successful at it was because of my support team's unwavering belief that I could learn to do things that my parents didn't think I could. Lou said I wouldn't understand about the care of a home, and the taxes and insurance fees and such. But I do, and did. All it took was Bill to explain it to me, slowly and carefully, and for my team to continue to teach and support me. So it was a matter of my team putting my desires at the center of the plan and finding a way to make it work for me. Let this also be a prompt for others to see how much folks can learn, instead of focusing on what they can't learn, or what you think they can't. And if they can't, then that's where a good support team comes into play. Everyone helping together to make life dreams successful!

I always knew what it was that I wanted. And yet, I lived under my parents' thumb. Romana has asked at what point I became totally determined to get my way, and I would have to say that it was after my nasal surgery. Before then, I was not really able to think clearly. I was always struggling for breath, and that took a lot of focus and I was also pretty depressed. Twenty-four hours a day I struggled to breathe. But after the surgery, that is when everything began to change for me mentally. I was not focused only on my breathing, and I was able to think of all the things I wanted in life instead. And I was able to focus on my dreams and getting away from my parents finally and for good.

One can't place too much importance on the power of positive thought and using it to create what you want out of life. It's also called "The Law of Attraction." I have always assumed that I would get what I wanted and that my life would turn out the way that I wanted it to. Some folks, if you asked them what they wanted in life, they would say "I don't know." But I always did. I'd had a dog who had seizures and died from it, and after that I wanted to be a vet so I could help other dogs. But that dream was not to be, so I came up with new dreams. I just had a few detours along the way, and after my breathing was fixed, all of this came into clearer view for me. I have been blessed as well in that most of the people that I have been surrounded by also believed in the power of positive thought. These people helped support me in those goals I most wanted to accomplish such as leading as "normal" a life as possible. Getting married, having a home, and a child.

Romana and I were talking about the only time that I can think of when I didn't have enough confidence that things would go the way that I wanted. And in that case, it was more about my confidence in the legal system. This is different from my own self-confidence, as I had no control over what the legal system would do to me. And that is when I finally met with Bruce Kimzey to do the paperwork to get my conservatorship changed. I was so terrified of what Lou would do when he found out that I was frozen with fear. But Romana made me tell her what my fear was, and Bruce was able to explain to me that it was not a problem and that there was a legal remedy to keep Lou from moving me against my will again. So even though I didn't have the fortitude for it, my support system did. And that is also an important element to have in one's life. Make sure your support system believes in and supports your dreams. Don't allow people in your life that will shoot them down. Make sure that you surround yourself with people that will focus on your abilities and not your disabilities. People who will help you manifest your dreams and desires. If this book has any theme besides that of my own self-determination, it is this: ***Don't let others dissuade you from what you want most in your life.*** There is truth to the saying that "when a door closes, a window opens." You just have to make sure you don't sit and feel sorry for yourself when something does fail. Make yourself get up and do something. It also helps to focus on someone less fortunate than yourself when you take a blow that seems like a severe loss. For me, after Danielle was taken away, it helped for me to focus on my friend Carla who had the brain tumor. Suddenly, the grief over my loss seemed less in the face of my friend facing death. And helping her certainly took my mind off of everything that had happened with Danielle. And after Carla passed, I was able to look not just up, but forward to the future and resume my goal of finding the right wife to have children with.

It's important to visualize what it is that you want. Use all of your mental faculties to do this. And most importantly, ***don't*** focus on why it can't happen. That's a sure way to either slow things or even stop them by being self-defeating. Many things in life are self-fulfilling prophecies. I have manifested everything in my life that I told Romana I wanted the first day we met and she asked me what I most wanted. A wonderful home, a life with a wonderful spouse, and an amazing child. Anywhere along the line, I could have listened to those who told me I couldn't do it. From my parents to those at the group home who told me I wouldn't make it on my own. Romana has asked me if it was hard for me to stay true to what I wanted, and I would say emphatically ***no***! I always knew what I wanted, and I fully expected to get it. And it has all happened, and it continues to and always will because I will never give up!

And so I would say to you, don't give up either! Make your dreams happen! Assume they will, and they will.

Another thing that I've learned along the way is that compassion is a very important thing. Since my accident, I've been called a variety of different names including spaz, retard, stupid, and idiot. These names *hurt*! They hurt your heart, and they hurt your soul. I've had many dear friends also called such names. A while back, a friend of mine with Down syndrome was called a "downy" by a teenage boy at McDonald's. It served no purpose but to hurt him. The teenager went out of his way to raise his voice so that my friend could hear it. Short of getting into a fight with the kid, there was nothing he could do but leave, which he did. Sometimes people use these words and have no idea of the pain they cause. Any given day, you can read it on the net or hear it on the street. These words are *not* appropriate adjectives! They *are* the same as a racial slur. If I could ask you to do one thing, it would be to stop this name-calling. If you are around someone who does it, tell them to stop. And if you do it, please, don't ever do it again. I can't tell you the pain and heartache it causes. Just using those words are cruel. They are not words with no emotion in them. Granted, I was hit by a truck and became this way, but there are many people born this way. Just because they may have some disabilities does not mean they don't have any feelings. In fact, I often think that people with a lower IQ have a higher EQ (Emotional Quotient). Feelings are not a matter of intelligence, they are a matter of feelings.

During the time I have been working on this book, there have been changes in my family structure. In March of 2004, Lou passed away. I had high hopes at the time that things would go smoother with my family, but it has not worked out quite that way. My mother has remarried a fairly nice man, and my twin sister has passed away. I always thought that things would get better after Lou's death, that it was he who kept my mother in the state of mind she was in about how he treated me, but that has not turned out to be so. I don't see my mother except for perhaps once or twice a year. We have nothing in common but blood it seems.

At a family gathering after Lou's death, Kelli gave all of my family members copies of the draft of this book for them to read. We had asked my mother to read it and to make some factual historical "corrections." In particular, dates of things that I didn't know or remember due to my accident. My mother appears to still have her own interpretation of reality . . . never minding the facts that I have tried to go by to a large degree from the ALTA and court files. And it makes me feel like a baby all over again, again, and again and again. Instead of being enlightening and helpful, she attacked Kelli for helping me give a voice to the thoughts and feelings I have harbored about my experiences all these years. Which is funny in an odd way, because it has been Romana helping me write the book, not Kelli, although Kelli has been of great help in editing it and recording it so I can listen to it when I want to. My mother called it "a vicious attack on a man I loved and respected." I never said that all of it was exactly the way things really were. The whole point of this book has been to express how I felt and thought. I never said that it was logical, at least not the feelings part. I have tried to stay as factual as I could based on the neutral records from both the courts and all the ALTA files that were copied. She says that it is "unfortunate that Todd doesn't remember the love, care, and therapy appointments which certainly helped in his recovery."

I don't remember them that well to be honest, but I deeply appreciated them then and now. It was a "sad, difficult, and emotionally-charged time in our family life," *but*, that does not negate how I *feel* about how Lou handled me and my money in latter years. Those *feelings* are valid! That is the part she does not seem to understand. In the few notes that she did make (her note says she stopped reading the book when she realized it was just an attack on Lou, about thirty-six pages into it). We all found it rather shocking that in regards to the letter Lou wrote threatening to lock me up, she underlined only the part about how it "worked" to keep me in line. It seems that the fact that Lou lied about the court threatening to put me in a locked facility doesn't matter, only the fact that the lie worked. And if he lied to me about that, what else did he lie to me about? She said that the mistakes were never made in the "dishonest and underhanded way that you have decided to tell history." Hmmmm . . . well . . . to me . . . lying to someone about the court threatening to put them in a locked facility is "dishonest and underhanded." There are unfortunately many such incidents along the way . . . Lou lying to Susie for instance about the fact that I had only gotten a small settlement and would have to live off of that . . . was also just one other lie. She calls this book a "diatribe" . . . well . . . perhaps it is in her opinion, but it is also my therapy . . . and how often does a therapist ask you about the facts? Rarely I think, most often therapy is about your feelings. And again, I *have* tried to be as factual as I can be. I have stood corrected many times as I have researched this book and sorted my "memories" from the facts wherever I have been able to find them.

One of the "corrections" that Roberta makes is directly contested by a court document (this is in regards to the early court settlement) where the driver and his brother were in the truck. She wrote that there "was no brother." Well, I didn't pull that out of my memory; that is **directly** from the court records, so I **know** she is wrong about that. So in the end, I can't use anything that she wrote, for it seems her memory is as faulty as mine; the difference is, I **know** mine is faulty and I accept factual corrections. She doesn't!

For many years, I fought Romana on giving Roberta the benefit of the doubt. I always hoped that when Lou died, that her loyalty would be to me, her son. But, from the tone of the note she sent back with the draft, I am sorry to say that I just can't do that anymore. She herself has laid to rest any hopes of mine that she might have stood up for me against Lou's behavior in the past, however well intended that they might have supposedly been. Her refusal to accept that my feelings about Lou had any validity have pretty much put the nails in the family coffin, at least as of this writing.

My sister Stephanie (to no surprise) has sided with Roberta and says that this book is a vicious attack on Lou. Cindy sent it back with no comments. Stephanie says that Lou was her role model for an honest and upright man. That he was the best man she ever knew and graded all others based on him. I will grant that her life experiences with him was very different than mine was. Perhaps she did not realize the vast array of mistruths that Lou told me and others along the way. Or his repeatedly blatant disregard for the court and the laws of how a conservatorship is supposed to be handled. He repeatedly refused to obey the law. How is that honest and upstanding, I ask you? Not just once, but twice he comingled my funds with that of him and my mother, something the court told him specifically **not to do**, but he still did. He lied to me about the court locking me up and denied me fair use of the funds given to me in the settlement by the city of Modesto for me to have a better quality of life. I had to fight him every step of the way in latter years for anything that I wanted, and he still refused, which is why the whole conservatorship battle ensued in the first place.

If he had allowed the communication device and a modest home for me, most likely none of this would have happened. If he has seen fit to visit me and explain things to me like an adult, then again, things might have been different. I would never have let him be my conservator again (that would have been just plain dumb on my part), but if he had at any time come and apologized for hurting me as he did, I would have forgiven him. I realize that my family disagrees with this book and that it is hard to read sometimes, but nonetheless . . . I am not above forgiving him if he had ever expressed regret for the things he did. But, as far as I can tell, my mother and sister are *not* willing to forgive me for expressing the thoughts and feelings I have had locked up for years . . . not allowing me the right to feel the way I have. And I find that tragic. This book was never meant to be an attack. It was meant to be my truth for others to learn from and to help avoid the very things that are still tearing my family apart, even now, going on four years after Lou's death. While they are allowed their feelings, it seems I am not allowed mine. I, however, refuse to be their victim anymore and will stand by what I have written.

In reflection of the above paragraphs, I'd like to sum it all up on a helpful note to those reading this, and that is how all this could have been avoided or changed so that the conflict wasn't so ugly at the end. In retrospect, if my family had been willing to participate in a "team meeting" where everyone could have brought their issues and concerns to the table and discussed them like rational adults, then much of this most likely could have been avoided. But that would also require an open mind and willingness to compromise. I would have been willing to give some if Lou had. I would have listened to the wisdom of my team, for they had much knowledge and training in the areas of independent living. And perhaps Lou would have seen how much I had grown and not thought of me only as the rebellious individual that he pigeonholed me as and not allowed me the grace to be the more flexible adult I was trying so hard to be.

Lou and my mother were certainly invited to participate in my team meetings over the years, but they chose not too. So it wasn't a matter of them not being asked. I would hope that in the future, this book will inspire families to unite and come together for the best of the individual and for the family.

Having had such a difficult conservatorship experience has inspired me to look into the existing laws and see where I might be able to affect some sort of change for the better. Romana says that it's probably fairly rare that someone comes out of being conserved when it's not just a temporary situation. I know what mistakes were most devastating to me and can speak to the issues as someone who has not just lived them, but been controlled and unfairly treated for many years. I have been very torn about the idea of writing about my mother and family quite so unvarnished, but

I do believe that in order to help others avoid the pitfalls that my family fell into, I have to share the most difficult parts of what we all went through.

In January of 2007, Governor Schwarzenegger signed into law the Omnibus Conservatorship and Guardianship Reform Act of 2006, which are in essence four different laws of sweeping conservatorship law change. It's a good start. In 2006, the LA Times published a series of articles about the widespread abuse and lack of oversight and enforcement of existing conservatorship law, and the need for change in the existing law as well. This led to the Judicial Council establishing a series of hearings around the state to dissertain the problems and offered solutions to these same abuses. Unfortunately, by the time I became aware of this, the input from the community aspect was over. However, I am determined to still be a part of the changes that are needed to make conservatorships a safer place for the vulnerable population that they serve.

In moving forward from here, my newest project is to work on helping bring into action the recommendations of the final conservatorship report by the Judicial Council. I have picked two areas to start with that I feel very strongly need to be changed and that I feel will have a maximum impact on conservatees, and that I feel would have helped avoid the situations that I found myself in. Primary among their recommendations that I would like to see enacted is the appointment of attorneys for *every* conservatee and also the conservatee's bill of rights. I feel I have much to offer as insight from my personal experience.

To quote the Final Conservatorship report:

Automatic appointment of counsel for conservatees

The task force recommends automatic appointment of counsel *for conservatees in all cases.* Conservatees are vulnerable members of society who have been placed under the control of a conservator with oversight duty placed squarely on the superior court. Our current justice system mandates the appointment of counsel where vulnerable parties and defendants risk the loss of liberty and property, not only minors under wardship of the court, but also criminal defendants, whether accused of a felony or misdemeanor. Conservatees are similarly vulnerable, if not more so. Their entire lives and dignities are in the hands of others, including where they live, what their money is spent on, who they see, where they travel, and what property they are allowed to possess. Under current law, the court has discretion to appoint an attorney for a conservatee, the costs of which are paid from the conservatee's assets, if possible, or at the expense of the county or court. To implement this recommendation to require appointment of counsel in every case, a feasibility study would have to be made and funding identified for those conservatees who could not afford the cost. In exploring this idea further, alternatives should be considered, such as "unbundling" of attorney services, allowing limited appearances for matters that require an attorney, or the development of a managed counsel program such as the Dependency Representation, Administration, Funding, and Training (DRAFT) project in the dependency counsel area. The task force realizes this recommendation may take years to implement, but the protections afforded to conservatees would be well worth the time and expense in quality of life, better oversight, and increased attention given to the conservatee.

And

Conservatee Rights and Protections
42. Written bill of rights for conservatees

A written bill of rights should be established for conservatees. It should include procedural rights of due process, including the right to contest the establishment of the conservatorship, the right to remove the conservator, the right to terminate the conservatorship, and the right to privacy as well as a clear statement that conservatees be allowed the greatest degree of freedom possible consistent with the underlying reasons for their conservatorships. The bill of rights should include direction to conservators to give as much regard to the wishes of conservatees as permissible under the circumstances so that they might function at the highest level their abilities permit. It should be clear that a conservator is required to give due regard to the preferences of the conservatee and to encourage the conservatee's participation in decision making. The bill of rights should be given to the conservatee and acknowledged by the conservator.

We have also decided to pursue a few things both with ALTA Regional Center and the Department of Developmental Disabilities in regards to conservatorships/guardians and the right to privacy. We also have some suggestions as to ways to improve services to those that have conservators, so that the things that happened to me and Danielle won't happen to other ALTA clients if we can help it.

So, these are some of the things that I plan to focus on the most, in addition to getting this book published.

Chapter 21

A Reflection on Danielle
(What we would do differently to save her)

This chapter is going to be written just a bit differently than the other ones. In this, both Todd and I (the one typing, Romana) will be expressing our thoughts and feelings about all that transpired with his ex-wife Danielle. If just one thing in all of this book would change any life, then this is one of those chapters that we both feel very strongly about. We have left this subject right to the very end on purpose, so it will be one of the last things you, the reader, are left with.

We will also be repeating things that we have mentioned before, but again, this is such an emotional subject to us, so we are saying it again on purpose. Last time was for us as part of the book; this time is for Danielle.

Todd says that he is exactly where he is supposed to be, living the life with his wonderful wife and child just as he is supposed to be. (And that, is absolutely true.)

And I say, yes, but there is one left behind, one who begged and pleaded with us to not let her be taken away, and that is Todd's former wife, Danielle.

I cannot tell you how many times over the past twelve years Todd and I have had this discussion. I have "lost" a client to a brain tumor, Todd's friend Carla who we wrote about earlier, but Danielle was taken from us. In spite of her pleas, and that always weighs heavy on my heart and on Todd's too.

Todd and I have discussed what we would do differently this time. And these are the things we have come up with.

First off, I would take her to Adult Protective Services and have her tell them what she was telling all of the staff at Choices and Todd's conservator, Bill Cody, and her volunteer from Choices, Valerie. In all, there were ten different individuals from three different agencies, along with Bill, the conservator, whom she spoke to in regards to her happiness in her marriage and her concerns about her parents being much too controlling and even to some of us of her fear of them coming and taking her back because they needed her money to keep their house and to please not let that happen. The APS investigator never spoke with any of the staff members who had been with her for the longest times and knew her the best and who were with her up to just a few days before she left.

Neither they would not listen to the ALTA caseworker who also told them she had grave concerns about the situation, and who had met alone with Todd and Danielle when called to their home by them to specifically address the issue of the parents' overcontrol. She was also at the meeting then held at ALTA, again, specifically in regards to Todd and Danielle's concerns about the parents.

The investigator said we were "too strong advocates for her."

(Romana says, "Personally I appreciated the compliment, as long as it's what the client wanted.")

Simultaneously, and if she would not go to APS then at the least, we would videotape the person saying what they did or didn't want to happen in a neutral environment with an attorney or some other witnesses, maybe ALTA and the local Area Board members, or Protection and Advocacy. There has to be *some* sort of backup for when that person is back in the abuser's control. I know abuser is a very strong word to use. But, if you take someone's whole life away, and all their dreams, mental and emotional, to be sure. Financial? Well, Danielle said one of the main reasons her parents were taking her back was because they couldn't make it without her SSI and the IHSS money that her mom got for taking care of her. What else would you call destroying your child's happy marriage for money? Because that's what it came down to. I have said it earlier in this book, and Todd and I both agree it bears repeating. Her parents did the very worst thing that any parent can do to their own child, and that is to use their disability against them as a weapon to control them. Todd lived this firsthand, and it still breaks his heart that Danielle is not living the life of freedom to choose her own path as he is now able to.

Romana says,

In the year and a half that I knew Danielle, she was always consistent about her feelings about her father and her desire to move as far away from him as she could. I will never forget his yelling at the mom about something in the dryer and feeling Danielle's hands cover my ears from behind me, and her intense embarrassment about her father's behavior and her almost frantic desire to leave the house as soon as possible. Or the feeling I'd get going there and her rushing me out of the house so that she could get away from him. She would be happy and relaxed while we were out, but jumpy as a cat in a room of rocking chairs when we got home. She had that feeling I know . . . of always being afraid of what is going to happen. Survival mode. Doing whatever it takes to appease the person. Another time, I remember she was closing her closet door, which was on a track, and it came off while she was closing it. Mr. Alexander came in and started yelling at her about it being broken and that now he was going to have to fix it *again*.

She spoke to him like a little girl and tried to appease him. We left immediately after that.

After she met Todd, in all the times I was with her alone, before and after the marriage, she never said anything about wanting to leave him. She loved him almost from the moment they met, and she would go on and on and on about him. She never once showed any fear of him, or spoke of being afraid of him or that he could not take care of her. She understood when he would get angry and pound on the countertop, often in regards to how her father treated her. She would wrap her arms around him and kiss him, and he would calm down and apologize, and she would say she understood and that they made her mad too. I never saw the fear in her then that I did when we were at her parents' house and I witnessed Mr. Alexander's angry outbursts.

One of the things she told her psychologist was that there wasn't enough healthy food in the house. Well, every month, since Todd had moved out on his own, we made a trip at the beginning of the month to Costco. Todd's parents had used that as a reason to move him home from Davis. They said that he didn't have any food in the house, so once he was on his own again, he always made sure there was a lot.

(The reality at that time of when Todd was living in Davis, is that he was working at the cafeteria and got all his meals there for free, so of course he ate the majority of his meals there and didn't need to keep much food at his place. This was especially true as Todd's father was only giving him $500 of his money at the time for his rent.)

Because of the fuss his parents had made in the past we made those monthly Costco trips where Todd would stock up on things. The Choices staff also took them shopping to the grocery store at least once a week, and her parents were there all the time checking and taking them to the store as well, so the reality is there was always an abundance of good food in their house, and her parents knew it. With three instructors looking out and checking in on everything, and taking them to lunch and shopping, not to mention her parents taking them shopping, there was no way that there was not enough food in the house.

Her psychologist was the only one to meet with Danielle alone (although her parents drove her there and then took her home, so one can only imagine the brainwashing of untruths that went on in the car on the way to that meeting). In that meeting, Danielle also said that although she loved Todd, she didn't see the marriage working. Why not? That is never clarified. She said that he hit her, but years later her father admitted to a mutual friend of one of the staff that "Todd had never done those things." That may or may not have been said, but we all knew that he hadn't. She also said that Todd couldn't help her manage her medications, but by then, he was doing very well with his own, far better than she. Todd did get scared for her a couple of times when she mistook her own meds incorrectly. That was one of the few times he did pound on the countertop as a result of her actions to impress her how dangerous it could be. He knew it was wrong, but she didn't at that moment. Todd also knew he would be blamed for it and that her parents were waiting for any opportunity to point out that the marriage wasn't working and to take her away. It's not something that was a surprise to us when it was used as a weak excuse for taking her back. But it was not a mortal sort of incident, and the next step would have been to have her meds locked up and given to her by Todd alone, as he never ever missed his meds. He always has an extra day of meds on his person as well, just to be sure; if he ended up away from home for some reason, he can cover them.

So he could certainly have been able to manage Danielle's meds.

Danielle's brain was like an old LP record with grooves in it, and every once in a while it would skip a few tracks and end up somewhere else that wasn't always reality. She might say for instance that she had no food, but if you showed her the cupboard with the food in it, she would then remember that it was there. If anything, perhaps we didn't know how many times it actually did skip before the marriage, but Todd was finding that out after and learning to compensate for it. Like locking up all the scissors in the house because she would use them to cut her eyebrows if she got her hands on them. There was certainly a reason that she had a psychologist. It had been not very many years since her accident, and she had many, many issues to deal with. Danielle could be very much like a chameleon and change her colors to suit the situation she was in. I believe this was a defense mechanism she learned to deal with her father to some degree. She could change to placate him very quickly.

I believe that this amazing and wonderful young woman has lost the life she wanted so much with Todd. But she is still alive, and while she is, there is still hope that somehow she might live that life she wanted of independence. I have never stopped grieving for her loss. And there is no way that it could not have been. Not only did she lose Todd, but she lost all of her other friends as well that she had made. She loved the women's group at Choices, and she loved time with her volunteer, Valerie. I know she enjoyed the time with her ILS instructors too, as we did with her. So she lost her home, husband, friends, and total support group. What a devastating blow that must have been. To be locked up and away from the freedoms that she had begun to experience.

I asked Todd what he would say to her if he could, and he signed that he hopes for her to find freedom and then a love of her own and a life of her own as she wants to live it. He is happy with his wife and daughter and wishes the same for her.

And I wish her the same. As we write this last part in September of 2009, the girl Jaycee Dugard was found eighteen years after she was kidnapped at eleven years of age. Reading this back and the life that Danielle has been living has something of a parallel to it. As Jaycee now celebrates her newfound freedom, so do I wish that Danielle might be free to blossom as she was beginning to do before she was snatched from those she loved and isolated from everyone. All her hopes and dreams that she shared with us have been locked away.

So, we write this, hoping it will somehow help. If not her, then perhaps others. If you know of anyone that you ever think might be in this position and you can do something about it, then for the sake of those that can't be freed, free who you can.

We hope this book may be a key that opens many cages.

Chapter 22

In Closing

I have high hopes for this book. It has become about much more than just my life. As we have written it, it has become about including all others who have been or may be like me, and the challenges there are to being disabled in this able-bodied/minded world. In the case of myself and others, it is often the mental capacity and divits where we need assistance over the bumpy parts. Everyone on the planet needs that from time to time.

I want to mention that in fact, I have totally forgiven Lou for all that he did to me, either or purpose or with the best of intentions. When I first found out that he was dead, I told Romana that he was in hell now. She said that I needed to forgive him, and how about if I made a deal with him. I looked at her, unsure of what she meant by that. She explained that she thought that I should give him a chance to redeem himself by helping make this book a success. That from the spiritual world, he could now reach out and touch in whatever way he can the hearts and minds of those that may have any influence in making this book reach as many people as possible to help them. So I readily agreed and it seems like a fair trade to me. I don't even feel mad at him anymore and even feel positive to some degree as we get ready to go to publishing. It is freeing to not be angry or hold a grudge against him. And forgiveness even for the worst of crimes makes it easier to move on with life with joy in your heart. Rage and blame just hold you down. I never forget what he did, and I am using this book to try and make sure that folks are enlightened so it that it will happen to less folks in the future. So, I am turning a negative, into a positive and I hope that the world can learn to forgive more as well.

Everything I have experienced and written just reaffirms that rising above your difficulties can be done. That also means recognizing we have them, and knowing that we all need help of one kind or another. We talked at lunch recently about the numbers in my life. The number of folks who hurt or tried to take advantage me or wrote me off was but a handful. The numbers who have helped me break free of my legal prison and begin fulfilling my truest purpose in life far outweigh those that sought to hinder me. All the staffs from all the places I have been placed or programs I have been in, I could never count. Or even the most simple of things. Like my moving heavy things for my friend, Dorothy Stearman, and her sewing the hem of my pants for me. Or the nice fella, Nate, who went out of his way to help us move an extra heavy TV we couldn't do alone. Folks helping folks with love. That's what matters the very most in this world!

We all go through cycles in this world, and if there is one thing I have also learned, it's the law of karma. That what goes around, does come around. Justice will be served. I am always amazed each time it happens yet again. If you help, then you are helped, although that is not the reason to help, it's just a nice side effect. And to those that do the opposite, here or there, their circle will come complete as well. I believe this with all my heart. But above all, I wish all love and joy and kindness to each other.

I hope this book will inspire everyone to be kind to each other and to be aware of the less fortunate among us, whatever that misfortune may be. Let's all give each other as much help and grace as we can. You never know when it might be your next. I never thought it would be me.

As was once said in a popular movie . . .

Be *excellent* to each other.

Index

Made in the USA
Charleston, SC
16 May 2011